TOD Herbal Kitchen

HOW TO COOK AND DESIGN WITH HERBS
THROUGH THE SEASONS

BaaHaus Design, Leslie Haines: Cover Design / Book Design
Mary Gunderson: Writer
Tamara Reynolds: Cover Photograph
Memphis Herb Society: Recipes / Information

TRADERY
H•O•U•S•E

Library of Congress Card Catalog Number: 95-61099
ISBN 1-879958-28-7

First Printing   1995
Second Printing   1997

For additional copies, use the order form in the back of the book, or call
The Wimmer Companies, Inc., 1-800-727-1034.

Printed in the USA by

WIMMER
The Wimmer Companies
Memphis

Memphis Herb Society

Formed in 1986, the Memphis Herb Society maintains an herb garden at the Memphis Botanic Gardens. Members gather monthly to share their appreciation of a group of plants that enriches their lives immeasurably. Because education is one of its major purposes, the society holds annual herb symposiums, bringing the country's leading authors and lecturers—such as Jim Wilson, Lucinda Hutson, Eone Riales, Josie Sides, Madalene Hill, Gwen Barclay, Adelma Simmons, Emelie Tolley, Tina Marie Wilcox— to Memphis to share their herb knowledge. There are so many good cooks in the society that the group published *A Thyme for Tea* in 1988 and

A Celebration of Herbs in 1991.

In *Today's Herbal Kitchen*, the Memphis Herb Society shares more wonderful recipes, crafts, tips, and herb expertise. Thanks to all the members who contributed material to us. And special thanks to Angela Mullikin, Helen Putnam, and Marie Brinn for their dedication to the project.

Special Thanks

Thanks also to food and garden writer Mary Gunderson for her informative, well-organized approach to the editorial material. Mary has written about herbs for national and regional magazines, for corporate clients, and for radio. She experiments in her own garden and kitchen in St. Paul, Minnesota.

Much appreciation goes to the creative talents of cover and book designer Leslie Haines. Leslie pursued an education and later a career in graphic design and advertising. With more than 11 years of experience in the field, she started her own business—BaaHaus Design in Nashville.

Table of Contents

Introduction

by Mary Gunderson

Herbs add the exotic, the extraordinary to your cooking. But herbs are nothing new in the kitchen. Sleek appliances, flavored coffees, and non-stick sprays: Your grandmother's mother would be amazed. Then, she'd see your herbs and she'd feel at home.

No doubt, she'd approve when you use herbs to experiment with new flavors or even to make her recipes better! *Today's Herbal Kitchen* is your guide to using herbs throughout the year. We've collected time-tested recipes and arranged them with the seasons. Among the recipes and ornamental ideas, you'll find herb basics and taste sensations for everyone around the table to enjoy. Recipes that help you in and out of the kitchen fast are marked:

Healthy cooking and herbs are a natural merger in the quest to cut fat and sodium. Many people don't miss either when herbs provide their own rich flavors. Throughout the book, we've marked those lighter recipes with the symbol:

The more you use herbs, the easier it is to understand why they've endured through centuries.

Herb History and Lore

The first garden plants to be coaxed from the wild and cultivated were herbs. Before long, herbs took their places in religion and mythology, where some were revered as symbols of new life (chervil), of victory in battle (dill), or of fidelity and friendship (rosemary).

Herbs were used in cooking, of course, especially valued for their power to minimize the flavor of bad meat in those days before refrigeration.

Across the globe in many cultures the herb garden was a trusted pharmacy and cosmetic counter. Herbs were the basis of potions, aphrodisiacs, teas, soothers for upset stomachs, and remedies for hair loss, wounds, plagues, and pestilence. Such fragrant herbs as lavender, mint, and thyme were often strewn on floors in cottages and castles to mask unpleasant odors. Many modern medicines and beauty prescriptive, in fact, are derived from herbs and other plants. Recent studies have confirmed some medicinal uses of herbs: Garlic is a natural antibiotic, for example. Mint in toothpaste is confirmed to whiten teeth.

Living With Herbs

Good things come in small measurements with herbs. Most herb recipes call for a teaspoon or less of one or two varieties meant to enhance, not overpower a dish. If herbs are new in your kitchen, start with small amounts and increase them until the taste suits you.

Take your pick of either fresh or dried herbs. Substitution is easy: *One tablespoon fresh, chopped herbs equals one teaspoon dried, a three-to-one ratio.* If you don't grow your own, many grocery stores stock at least fresh chives, parsley, garlic, and basil. Herb flavor lies in each plant's oils. To release them, chop fresh herbs finely just before cooking. For dried herbs, either pulverize with a mortar and pestle or crush between your fingers to release oils. The mortar and pestle is handy for combining herbs, as well.

Herbal Mix and Match

The sheer variety of herbs is one factor that makes the herbal kitchen so satisfying. But when you're first cooking with herbs, selection of which flavor with what food can be challenging. As a basic guide, think of herbs in these categories: strong-flavored, moderate-flavored, and delicate. Add strong-flavored herbs early in cooking to give flavors plenty of time to blend. Delicate herbs add more flavor if they're used near the end of cooking time. Their flavor disappears during long cooking times. Stir in or sprinkle on moderate-flavored herbs any time during cooking.

Strong-flavored herbs:
Bay leaf, caraway, fennel, sweet marjoram, oregano, rosemary, sage, savory, thyme.

Moderate-flavored herbs:
Chive, dill, mint.

Delicate herbs:
Basil, chervil, cilantro, parsley.

In this book you'll find dozens of ideas for making a place for herbs in your life. Herbs only increase your pleasures as you stir them into quick recipes for fast weekday suppers or bake them into such desserts as cheesecakes and cookies where herbs are an unusual and welcome addition. Your herbal kitchen awaits.

Herb Glossary

	Characteristics	Uses
Basil	(annual) Fresh basil has a licorice-spice taste. When dried, the flavor leans toward lemon and anise. Varieties vary in taste and fragrance, but are interchangeable in most recipes.	Good with tomatoes in any form, also pasta, pestos, fish, shrimp, duck, lamb, veal, venison, cabbage, carrots, onions, squash and beans, salad dressings, soups.
Chives	(perennial) From the Latin for "onion," appropriate because of chives' slightly sweet, light onion flavor. Both common types, chives and garlic chive are best fresh and can be frozen but don't dry successfully.	Chop for soft cheese, vegetables, herb mixtures, salads and dressing, omelets, cheeses, soup, and with fish.
Coriander or Cilantro	(annual) Probably native to Asia, but used by Egyptians to cure headaches. Leaves have a soapy, astringent taste. Orange-cumin-anise flavor of seeds is more widely accepted than that of leaves.	Leaves: Mexican and Chinese cooking. Seeds: biscuits, poultry stuffing, apple pie, meats, sausage, breads, cookies, pea soup, vinegar, salads, mustards, fish sauce, eggs and mushrooms, pickles, salads and soups.
Dill	(annual) Sweet, full aroma and cluster of pale yellow flowers. Lovely in garden planted with marigolds. Seeds delicious fresh or dried. Stems and leaves (dillweed) are used fresh, frozen, or dried.	Used in pickled cucumbers and other vegetables. Seeds also good in breads and apple desserts, as well as pasta, coleslaw, potato salad and cream soups. Fresh, chopped dillweed goes with fish. Mix dill with butter or yogurt to top vegetables or pasta. Stir into scrambled eggs.
Fennel	(annual) From same family as dill with similar look. Used as victory garland in ancient Greece. Licorice flavor is strongest in seeds. Fennel freezes well but loses most of its flavor when dried. Seeds, leaves, and bulbs all used in cooking.	Mixed with thyme and parsley in herb butter for fish or with rosemary and garlic for roast pork. Stir into breads, cakes, pastries, any apple dish, sauces, and soups. Good in lentil and dried bean dishes. Seeds are familiar as a main seasoning in Italian sausage.
Garlic	(annual) Recent studies have confirmed garlic's power as a natural antibiotic. Store whole bulbs in a cool, dry place and prepare fresh cloves as needed. Paper sheath comes off easily if you mash the garlic with the flat side of a knife first. Garlic is strongest when first cut or mashed and used raw. The inner core is more bitter and may be removed before using in dips or salad dressing. Garlic mellows when baked, fried, or stewed.	Use for sauces, dressings, meats, fish, poultry, tomato, and green vegetables. Rub a cut clove on the surface of a salad bowl before adding tossed salad. Add after browning onions for soups and stews. Sprinkle browned garlic over fresh, cooked vegetables.
Marjoram	(tender perennial) The name of this popular herb comes from the Greek meaning "delight of the mountains." The velvet-smooth leaves are delicious fresh; marjoram can be both frozen and dried successfully.	Good with any robust-flavored foods: Butter sauce for fish; in beef, lamb and pork dishes, cheeses, chopped meats, soups, meat loaf, stews, potatoes, pasta, rice, and vegetables.

	Characteristics	Uses
Mint	(perennial) A Greek writer claimed that the smell alone of mint refreshes our spirits. Mint comes in unusual flavors beyond spearmint and peppermint: apple, orange, lemon, chocolate, and pineapple. It's best fresh.	Use fresh leaves in fruit and vegetable salads, Middle Eastern recipes, garnish for summer's creamy fruit soups. Spearmint goes well with lamb in mint jelly. Fresh garden peas are lovely with a hint of mint. Rub a chicken with mint before roasting.
Oregano	(perennial): Soared to popularity in the United States after World War II probably due to the nation-wide acceptance of pizza. It's related to marjoram, but considered an old Spanish herb whose name is derived from "joy of the mountain." It's delicious fresh and retains flavor well when dried or frozen.	Many Spanish and Mexican dishes call for oregano. Stir it into meats, beans, sauces, soups, and use it with lamb and fresh mushrooms. Oregano enhances dishes with tomato, eggs, or cheese.
Parsley	(hardy biennial) For a continuous supply, plant each year. Parsley belongs to the carrot family, but in this case the greens are valued more than the root. One of our oldest cultivated plants, its uses extend far beyond plate garnish. Parsley is best fresh or frozen.	Stir into soups, sauces, egg dishes, salads, mashed potatoes, and marinades. Sprinkle chopped parsley over hot cooked rice, vegetables, pasta, and potatoes.
Rosemary	(tender perennial) The dusky, tender spikes (named in Latin, "dew of the sea") have potent flavor and aroma. There are both the tender prostrate and upright varieties. Rosemary can be used fresh or frozen and retains flavors well when dried.	Delicious in biscuits and breads, soups, eggs, poached fish, meats, poultry, basting sauces, and poultry.
Sage	(perennial) Sage has long represented health, wealth, and long life. "How can a man die who has sage in his garden?" questions an Arab proverb. In cooking, its strong flavors need to be used with a light hand. Sage is delicious fresh and dries well.	Classic in Thanksgiving's poultry stuffing. Rub on outside of lamb, pork, or beef roast or use in cold meat salads, cooked dried beans and lentils, cheeses and dips. Good with fennel for fish, veal, and sausage.
Tarragon	(perennial) There are two varieties: Russian and French. Russian has little or no flavor and is considered to be more of a weed. Herb experts prefer French tarragon. Both dried and frozen tarragon retain good flavors for cooking.	Try in salad dressings or with eggs. Good with poached fish, cooked vegetables, preserves, pickles, mustards, and vinegar. Sprinkle over sautéed meats or over meats and poultry before roasting or grilling.
Thyme	(annual) High praise in ancient Athens was to hear, "You smell of thyme." The sweet fragrance symbolized activity, courage, grace, and elegance. Thyme is another strong herb to be used judiciously, but widely.	Adds fine flavor to chowders, marinades, eggs, tomato sauce, all meats and poultry, pasta, rice, and most vegetables, especially potatoes, mushrooms, and tomatoes.

Grow Your Own Herbs

If you have a garden, you have room for herbs.

No matter if that patch of earth is an expanse of your yard or a few pots on the balcony, herbs give the garden a riot of fragrance and texture, a soothing contrast to brilliant-colored flowers. Because herbs are decorative as well as edible, they often grace borders and are planted as ground cover or accents in a rock garden or between stepping stones.

Border plantings make them easy to reach for cutting. Grow herbs amidst vegetables, especially planting those side-by-side that will be used together in recipes: basil near tomatoes and dill near cucumbers, for example. Place dill and coriander between tomatoes, cabbage, and broccoli.

Most herbs grow best in a sunny to partly sunny spot with at least six hours of sunlight a day. Plant them in soil with good drainage; water regularly and thoroughly. Herbs thrive in high humidity and like cool nights with temperatures under 60° F. Most herbs produce the strongest flavors when they aren't regularly fertilized. Mint is a notorious creeper. Better to sink a mint plant in a pot in the ground or plant in containers.

Grow the herbs you'd most like to use for cooking. Certain herbs lend themselves to special uses:

• If you garden indoors near a sunny window, good choices are sweet marjoram, thyme, parsley, winter savory, and chive.

• Hanging baskets or large pots are inviting with herbs trailing over the sides. Try basil, chives, or parsley in the middle, edged with rosemary, or creeping thyme.

• Classic herb gardens may have such formal designs as an interlocking knot. Or herbs can be arranged to cascade around rocks for a more naturalized herb garden.

• Plant containers with most ingredients needed for one dish. A spaghetti sauce garden places thyme, sweet marjoram, parsley, and oregano together. For salad gardens, combine lettuce, chives, lovage, parsley, and basil.

• Grow a tea garden! Use leaves from any mint, sage, chamomile, and lemon balm.

We've detailed herb harvest and preservation on page 12. The herb guide (page 8) notes which herbs are annuals and which are perennial. When gardening season ends, annual herbs are harvested and then pulled up by the roots. In colder climates, bring tender perennials, such as rosemary, indoors in pots and place in a sunny window.

Reaping the Harvest Year Round

How To Harvest, Preserve, and Store Herbs

The herb harvest is the beginning of good eating. Clip leafy, well-branched herbs. Some sources say flavor oils are strongest in herbs picked before the heat of the day, but many herb growers don't notice a difference in flavor quality when herbs are picked under hot sun or later. Most herbs can be picked throughout the growing season. Basil gives several harvests if it's not allowed to bloom. You can prolong the season by pinching off flower buds, but when herbs do bloom, the flowers are lovely garnishes for soups, salads, and sauces. Cilantro offers just one crop of leaves per seed whether or not you pinch off the flowers.

Keeping Herbs

Fresh-cut herbs: Dry thoroughly but gently, and then wrap them loosely in damp paper towels. Place in loosely closed plastic bag. Will keep a week a more.

Frozen herbs: Store in sealed and marked plastic bags for about six months.

Dried herbs: Store in cool, dry, dark place, away from stove or appliance that gives off heat. For best flavor, use within six months.

Preserving Herbs

When herbs are preserved, they become the timeless seasonings favored by so many cultures around the globe. They're easy to dry or can be frozen or preserved in vinegar.

Start the process just after harvest. Rinse herbs quickly in water at room temperature and lightly blot them dry or whirl in a salad spinner.

To dry herbs and their flowers for bouquets or wreaths, treat them with an agent (borax powder, builder's sand, or glycerin) to retain color and shape. These herbs are no longer edible.

For cooking herbs, choose from several drying methods for single herbs or group herbs according to your taste. These herb combinations are tantalizing for recipes or gifts.

Substitutions:

3 teaspoons (1 tablespoon)
fresh herbs =
1 teaspoon dried herbs

Fines herbs: Classic French blend of fresh tarragon and chervil that may include parsley and chives. Added at end of cooking time or sprinkled on egg, cheese, and fish dishes

Bouquet garni: Another classic mixture, this one of bay leaf, thyme, celery leaves, and parsley tied in cheesecloth

or packed in a tea ball during simmering of soups and stews.

Basic herb mix: Combine one part each chives and parsley along with one or two robust-flavored herbs such as tarragon, basil, sweet marjoram, thyme, or savory

Preservation Methods

1. **In the bag**: Hang in bunches: those that dry quickly: savory, sage, mint, oregano, rosemary. Tie cut stems in a bunch and hang upside down. If it's dusty, enclose herbs in a paper bag punched with holes. Hang in a warm dry place with good air circulation and out of direct sun for about two weeks. Handle and crumble herbs as little as possible. More flavor oils are retained in whole leaves. Strip crisp leaves into airtight jars or bags and store in a cool dry place.

2. **On a tray:** On stacked frames stretched with mesh or cheesecloth, make single layers of rinsed, dried herbs. Allow at least an inch or two between trays. Most herbs will dry in seven to ten days. Gently turn herbs for even drying.

3. **In the oven:** Make a single layer of herbs on a baking sheet. Set oven at lowest setting and leave sheet in oven for 10 to 30 minutes with oven door open. Turn herbs gently for even drying. Remove when dry to touch to retain oils.

4. **Seed heads:** Pick mature seed heads when still green. Otherwise seeds may scatter from plant before you have a chance to harvest them. Bundle stems with seedheads upside down in a paper bag punched with holes in sides. Seeds will be caught as they dry. Dry thoroughly, about two weeks, and store in airtight jars or bags.

5. **In the microwave:** Rinse and dry as above. Microwave semi-dry herbs layered evenly, not stacked, on paper towels. Microwave on HIGH for 2 to 4 minutes per cup of herbs. Watch closely and mix or rearrange every 30 seconds. Remove from oven and cool on paper toweling. If not crumbly when cool, continue drying 15 to 30 seconds at a time. If using less than 1 cup herbs, reduce cooking time accordingly starting with HIGH for 1 minute, stirring every 15 seconds.

6. **In the freezer:** Best for tender herbs: basil, chives, dill, fennel, parsley, and tarragon. Rinse and pat herbs dry. Freeze whole leaves in plastic bags up to one year. Use in place of fresh herbs in cooking, but herbs may not be attractive for garnishes. Or, place a few herbs in each compartment of an ice cube tray. Cover with water and freeze. Combine frozen cubes in plastic bag. Drop in soups, stews, or sauces or thaw slightly, chop partially frozen herbs, and use in any other recipe, except as garnish.

Herb Vinegars

The taste of any vinegar infused with an herb is subtle, but unmistakable.

Throughout the year, you will find herb vinegar gives fresh harvest taste to salad dressings, marinades, and sauces. These are easier to prepare than you may have thought.

Start with good quality wine or rice vinegar. The better vinegar you begin with, the better quality your steeped vinegar will be. Rinse and thoroughly dry herbs (gently pat dry or use salad spinner) before stuffing them into a glass jar or bottle. Steep herbs in quart jars, for example, and decant to decorative bottles for storage or gifts. Choose one of three methods for the vinegar:

• To draw the most flavor from herbs, heat vinegar to just below boiling point and pour over herbs. Store in cool, dry place for about six weeks, stirring mixture daily.

• Or, place herb-stuffed vinegar bottles in the sun, covering bottles with mesh or cheesecloth to discourage insects. Vinegar is ready in about four weeks.

• If you'd rather not heat herbs, combine herbs and vinegar in bottles and let stand four to six weeks in cool, dark place.

After steeping, strain herb vinegar into decorative bottles and tuck a sprig of the appropriate fresh herb into each for a nice appearance and continued flavoring. Close bottle with a cork or with waxed paper and a metal screw-top lid. Store in a cool, dark place until needed.

Delicious Combinations

Red wine vinegar:
• sage, parsley, shallots

White wine vinegar:
• borage, dill, shallots
• mint, honey, cardamom seed
• dill, nasturtium blossom
• savory, chive blossoms
• fennel leaf, garlic, parsley
• lemon verbena, lemon basil, lemon thyme, lemon grass, lemon peel

Cider vinegar:
• chiles, garlic, oregano

Rice vinegar:
• rose and violet petals

Champagne vinegar:
• orange peel, orange mint

Herb Oils

Food safety is the first consideration in making herb oils.

Herbs are among the low-acid foods (garlic, mushrooms, and chili peppers are others) that can be a source of the bacteria *Clostridium botulinum*. The bacteria is commonly found in soil, air and water, but becomes deadly when stored in an oxygen-free medium such as oils. Commercially prepared herb oils are safe because they are adequately heat-processed. Herb oils prepared at home are at risk to promote growth of *Clostridium botulinum* and other spoilage bacteria that can cause illness or death.

These guidelines will help you prepare and use herbs in oil safely.

1. As a general rule store herbs or garlic in oil no longer than three weeks for best flavor quality and to minimize growth of those bacteria that will continue to grow under refrigeration temperatures.

2. Dried herbs or dried garlic in oil can be stored safely at room temperature because water isn't present to promote bacterial growth.

How To Make Herbed Oils:

Use a ratio of ½ cup finely chopped herbs with 1 cup oil. Shake well or mix in blender. Use immediately or refrigerate up to three weeks.

Herb & Oil Combinations

Olive oil:
- oregano, thyme, garlic
- basil, chili peppers, garlic
- lovage, garlic, celery leaf
- lemon basil, lemon thyme, rosemary

Peanut oil:
- chervil, tarragon, shallots

Sunflower oil:
- dill, garlic

Walnut oil:
- lemon verbena, lemon thyme

Safflower oil:
- fresh ginger, cardamom seed, coriander leaf

Please Eat These Flowers

Blossoms and flowers from herbs are not only lovely to look at. They add flavor and color in cooking. Besides the obvious use of garnishes, toss edible flowers with salads and stir into stir-fries.

The key to edible flowers is using only those that you are sure are safe to eat and those that haven't been sprayed with pesticides. If buying from a grower or market, ask how the plants were raised and avoid those that have been sprayed. Throughout the growing season there's a selection of blossoms and flowers. Pick them at their peak. Gently rinse and dry them. Use immediately or store in loosely closed plastic bag in the refrigerator.

Ways With Edible Flowers

• Apple blossoms and tulip leaves are the earliest edible offerings.

• Through late spring and summer pick flowers from begonias, calendulas, chives, daylilies, gladiolus, lilac, marigolds, mint, nasturtium, pansies, rose bushes and squash.

• Wrap chicken salad in daylily petals or float chive blossoms on cold potato soup.

• Sprinkle a few blossoms from roses or pansies on the bottom of a cake pan before pouring in batter.

• Adorn pastries and fancy desserts with candied flowers that have been dipped in sugar syrup (boil and cool syrup first).

• Arrange an edible centerpiece with flowers, vegetables, and fruits and invite everyone to munch.

Edible Flowers	Poisonous Flowers
bee balm	azalea
begonias	amaryllis
calendula (pot	buttercup
marigold)	bird-of-paradise
chrysanthemums	clematis
daylilies	daffodil
dianthus	delphinium
(pinks)	foxglove
fruit tree	hydrangea
blossoms	iris
garden peas	lily-of-the-valley
(not sweet	lupine
peas)	monkshood
geraniums	oleander
honeysuckle	poinsettia
lilac	rhododendron
marigold	sweet pea
(lemon	tansy
gem)	wisteria
nasturtium	
roses	
squash	
blossoms	
tulips	
violet family	
(including	
pansy)	

Herbs in Spring

With its warming days and soothing rains, spring is a day-to-day promise of everything light and fresh. Our cooking turns to tender spring vegetables and to lighter meals to help shake off the weight of winter. Fresh herbs begin to be more readily available, contributing a sense of nature's blessings to the season's meals.

Herbs in Spring

Invite friends and set the table for tea. Fresh herbs with fruit can be the basis of zesty spreads on tender quick breads, crackers or mildly sweet rolls. Pass herbed cookies and drop slices of mint in each tea cup. Pour the tea and pass the conversation.

A dish of bitter herbs, often horseradish in the United States, is passed during the Passover meal as a reminder of the bitterness of slavery in Egypt. If you live in a mild climate, oregano comes back early in the garden and can be one of the first to return fresh to your cooking.

At spring yard and garage sales, begin to collect decorative bottles to be cleaned and filled with herb vinegar in the fall.

Appetizers, Beverages, Etc.

Marinated Shrimp

1. Cook shrimp, lemon juice, lemon rind, and bay leaves in boiling water. Drain and place in a container.

2. Combine capers and next 8 ingredients to make a marinade. Pour marinade over shrimp. Add onion. Refrigerate overnight, shaking several times to redistribute marinade.

3. Drain shrimp. Serve on a lettuce-lined platter with toothpicks on the side. Garnish.

Yield: 20 to 24 servings

5 pounds fresh shrimp, peeled and deveined
Juice and rind of 1 lemon
4 dried bay leaves
1 (3-ounce) jar capers, undrained
2½ cups salad oil
1 cup dill or red wine vinegar
2 tablespoons celery salt
1 tablespoon onion powder
1 tablespoon black pepper
1 tablespoon Worcestershire sauce
2 teaspoons sugar
Dash of hot pepper sauce
2 medium-size sweet onions, chopped
Sprigs of fresh parsley for garnish

Spring

Deviled Eggs With Herbs

12 hard-cooked eggs
⅓ cup mayonnaise
2 tablespoons honey
   mustard with
   raspberries
½ teaspoon garlic
   dill vinegar
½ teaspoon dried dill
½ teaspoon dried
   thyme
½ teaspoon salt
   Black pepper and
   cayenne pepper
   for garnish

1. Slice eggs in half lengthwise and carefully remove yolks. Mash yolks with mayonnaise.

2. Add mustard and next 4 ingredients. Mix well. Spoon yolk mixture into egg whites. Sprinkle with peppers.

Yield: 12 servings

Orange Toast

1 stick margarine,
   softened
½ cup sugar
2½ teaspoons fresh or
   dried orange zest
1 tablespoon
   chopped fresh
   mint
1 loaf thinly sliced
   white bread, crusts
   removed

1. Cream margarine and next 3 ingredients. Spread on bread.

2. Stack slices and cut with an electric knife or a sharp knife into thirds. Separate slices and place on a greased baking sheet.

3. Bake at 325° for 15 to 20 minutes.

Yield: 24 to 30 servings

Tiny rosebuds can be frozen in ice cubes to adorn warm-weather drinks.

Lemon Butter

 1. Beat eggs. Slowly beat in remaining ingredients.

2. Cook in a double boiler until thickened, stirring constantly. Cool. Store in refrigerator.

Yield: about 1½ cups

This recipe is great on toast or waffles and also makes a good filling for layer cakes.

3 eggs
1 cup sugar
5 tablespoons butter, melted
Zest and juice of 2 lemons
Finely chopped fresh lemon balm or citrus mint to taste

Orange Spread

 1. Cream all ingredients until thoroughly mixed.

2. Spread on toast or loaf breads.

Yield: about 1 cup

1 stick butter
3 tablespoons orange juice
3 tablespoons sugar
2 tablespoons orange zest
Ground coriander or nutmeg to taste

Watercress Spread

 1. Combine first 6 ingredients in a saucepan. Heat and stir until thickened.

2. Serve very hot on buttered toast. Garnish with watercress sprigs.

Yield: about ½ cup

1 bunch watercress, minced
2 tablespoons cream
1 egg, beaten
1 tablespoon butter
Dash of lemon juice
Salt and pepper to taste
Sprigs of fresh watercress

Spring

Middle Eastern Relish

1 cup peeled and chopped cucumber

3 chopped radishes

Fresh chives or scallions

Rice wine vinegar

Sugar to taste

1. Combine all ingredients and let stand several hours or overnight.

2. Serve as an accompaniment to meats.

Yield: 6 to 8 servings

A simple way to use spring's early gifts of radish and chives.

Tarragon Mustard

2 teaspoons dried tarragon, divided

¼ cup mustard seed

¼ cup dry white wine

⅓ cup white wine vinegar

⅓ cup water

⅛ teaspoon black pepper

⅛ teaspoon ground allspice

2 teaspoons honey

1 teaspoon salt

1. Mix together 1 teaspoon tarragon and next 3 ingredients. Let stand 3 hours.

2. Combine mixture with water and next 4 ingredients in a food processor or blender. Process until pureed.

3. Transfer mixture to the top of a double boiler. Stir over simmering water 10 minutes or until thickened. Cool.

4. Mix in remaining 1 teaspoon tarragon. Place in a jar, cover, and refrigerate.

Yield: about 1½ cups

Mustard from "scratch" is easy in the food processor.

Herbal Vinaigrette

 1. Combine all ingredients in a food processor and blend.

2. Bottle and refrigerate for future use.

Yield: about 4 cups

Add different herbs according to personal taste preferences.

2   cups wine or cider vinegar
1   cup water
½   cup virgin olive oil
Fresh lemon juice
2   large cloves garlic, pressed
2   tablespoons sugar
Salt to taste
½   jalapeño pepper
½   cup fresh parsley
½   cup fresh basil

Honey and Green Onion Dressing

 1. Place green onion and next 4 ingredients in a food processor. Blend for 2 minutes.

2. Continue to process while slowly adding oil.

Yield: about 1 cup

3   green onions, coarsely chopped
3   tablespoon herbal red wine vinegar
2   tablespoons honey
2   tablespoons medium picante sauce
2   dashes black pepper, or to taste
⅓   cup olive or canola oil

Spring

Herb Dressing

¾ cup extra virgin olive oil
2 tablespoons minced onion
1 clove garlic, minced
2 tablespoons freshly grated Parmesan cheese
1 tablespoon minced fresh basil
½ teaspoon crumbled dried oregano leaves
¼ teaspoon dry mustard
½ teaspoon sugar or honey
¼ teaspoon salt
¼ teaspoon freshly ground black pepper
1 tablespoon balsamic red wine vinegar
1 tablespoon fresh lemon juice

1. Combine oil and next 9 ingredients in a blender or food processor. Blend for 30 seconds.

2. Add vinegar and lemon juice. Blend for 30 seconds or until well combined. Taste and adjust flavor as desired, using extra seasonings, vinegar, or lemon juice.

Yield: about 1½ cups

This dressing tastes best within 24 hours of preparation. The garlic and onion flavors become too strong if held longer.

In the Middle Ages, sage tea was a spring tonic for many people.

Amish Friendship Bread

1. On first day, combine ½ cup sugar, ½ cup flour, and ½ cup milk in a plastic or glass bowl. Mix well. Do not use a metal utensil and do not refrigerate.

2. On second, third, and fourth days, stir mixture.

3. On the fifth day, mix in 1 cup sugar, 1 cup flour, and 1 cup milk.

4. On the sixth through the ninth day, stir mixture. On the tenth day, complete starter mix by adding remaining 1 cup sugar, 1 cup flour, and 1 cup milk. Mix well.

5. To make bread, combine 1 cup of starter mix with oil and next 3 ingredients. Combine flour and next 8 ingredients in a separate bowl. Add to wet ingredients and mix well. Stir in nuts.

6. Pour into two well-greased loaf pans or a well-greased Bundt pan. Bake at 325° for 60 minutes or until a toothpick inserted in the center comes out clean.

Yield: *4 cups starter mix and 2 loaves bread*

Divide leftover starter mix into 1 cup portions and give to friends (along with the bread recipe), or freeze.

Starter Mix

2½	cups sugar, divided
2½	cups all-purpose flour, divided
2½	cups milk, divided

Bread

1	cup starter mix
½	cup oil
1	cup milk
3	eggs
1	teaspoon vanilla
2⅓	cups all-purpose flour
1	teaspoon ground rosemary or coriander
1	(5.1-ounce) package instant vanilla pudding mix
1	cup sugar
1½	teaspoons baking powder
2	teaspoons cinnamon
	Dash of nutmeg
½	teaspoon salt
½	teaspoon baking soda
1	cup walnut pieces

Flaxseed Bread

Flaxseed Meal

1½-2   cups flaxseed

Bread

3½-4   cups bread flour, divided

2   cups flaxseed meal

2½   cups whole wheat flour

1   (¼-ounce) package active dry yeast

1   teaspoon salt

2¾   cups hot water

1½   tablespoons canola oil

½   cup honey

1. To make flaxseed meal, process flaxseed in a blender until the consistency of cornmeal.

2. Prepare bread by combining 2 cups bread flour and next 4 ingredients. Combine water, oil, and honey, being sure temperature does not exceed 130°. Stir into dry ingredients. Mix well. Add enough of remaining bread flour to make a soft dough.

3. Turn dough onto a floured surface and knead 6 to 8 minutes or until smooth and elastic. Add extra bread flour as needed. Form into 2 loaves. Place in 9x5-inch loaf pans coated with nonstick cooking spray.

4. Spray top of dough and cover. Let rise in a warm place for 60 minutes to 1 hour, 30 minutes. Bake at 350° for 40 to 45 minutes or until browned and hollow sounding when tapped. Remove from pans and cool on a rack.

Yield: 2 loaves

 Flax is usually planted as a grain and harvested for its oil, called linseed, and its fibers that are woven into linen. But in much of the world it has long been held in regard as a medicinal herb and as part of the human diet. Look for the nutty flavored seeds in some supermarkets or natural foods stores.

Herb Sour Cream Bread

1. In a large bowl, combine 3½ cups flour and next 6 ingredients.

2. Heat sour cream, water, and margarine in a saucepan until hot to the touch. Stir into dry ingredients. Add eggs. Mix in only enough of remaining 1 cup flour to make batter stiff. Cover and let stand 10 minutes.

3. Stir down batter. Pour into two greased 1-quart casserole dishes. Sprinkle with sesame seeds. Cover and let rise in a warm, draft-free place 30 to 40 minutes or until doubled in size.

4. Bake at 375° for 30 to 35 minutes. Remove from pans and cool on racks.

Yield: 2 loaves

4½ cups all-purpose flour, divided
⅓ cup sugar
1 teaspoon salt
½ teaspoon dried thyme
½ teaspoon dried marjoram
½ teaspoon dried oregano
2 (¼-ounce) packages quick-rising active dry yeast
1 cup sour cream
½ cup water
6 tablespoons margarine
2 eggs, room temperature
Sesame seeds

Spring

Banana Punch

5   bananas
4   cups sugar
6   cups water,
     divided
1   (46-ounce) can
     pineapple juice
1   (12-ounce) can
     frozen orange
     juice concentrate
2   cups lemon juice
1   (2-liter) bottle
     lemon-lime
     carbonated drink
Fresh mint of choice
     for garnish

1. Mash bananas with a fork. Heat and stir sugar and 2 cups water until sugar dissolves.

2. Combine banana, sugar mixture, remaining 4 cups water, and next 3 ingredients. Pour into a 1-gallon jug and freeze.

3. Remove from freezer a few hours before serving. Thaw to a slush consistency and transfer to a punch bowl. Add carbonated drink. Garnish.

Yield: about 18 to 20 servings

Coffee Choco-mint Punch

2   quarts strong
     coffee, cold
2   cups milk
½   cup sugar
2   teaspoons vanilla
1   quart vanilla ice
     cream
Whipped cream
Sprigs of fresh
     chocolate mint

 1. Combine coffee and next 3 ingredients. Mix well.

2. Place ice cream in a punch bowl. Pour coffee mixture over top.

3. Add a dollop of whipped cream and a sprig of chocolate mint to each serving.

Yield: 18 servings

For a spring brunch, surprise guests with this coffee float finished with the unexpected—a sprig of chocolate mint.

Fruit Juice Icy Cooler

2 (16-ounce) packages frozen strawberries
1 (15¼-ounce) can crushed pineapple
2 bananas, thinly sliced
1 (6-ounce) can frozen orange juice concentrate
1 (6-ounce) can frozen lemonade concentrate
2 cups water
1 cup sugar
2 tablespoons finely chopped fresh lemon balm
2 tablespoons finely chopped fresh mint

1. Combine all ingredients and freeze.

2. Thaw 2 hours before serving to achieve an icy consistency.

Yield: 8 to 10 servings

Springtime Potpourri

1 cup whole star anise
2 cups lemon verbena leaves
1 cup pansy flowers
2 cups geranium flowers and leaves
4 cups rose petals
2 cups other blooming flowers
1 cup orange peel cut in small pieces
1 cup oak moss
5 drops orange oil
5 drops rose oil
5 drops floral oil (any selection)

1. Dry all plants and orange peel until crisp. Mix together well.
2. Add oils to oak moss. Mix all ingredients together.
3. Store in airtight glass container for 2 weeks; then use in open bowls and baskets.

Spring

Sorrel Soup

4   potatoes
1   cup fresh French
    sorrel leaves
6   leeks, 4 shallots, or
    1 medium onion,
    chopped
1   clove garlic
    crushed
3   tablespoons butter
6   cups chicken broth
1   sprig rosemary, or
    chopped fresh
    parsley or chives
    for garnish

1. Boil potatoes until tender. Peel and cube.

2. Sauté sorrel, leek, and garlic in butter until soft but not browned. Add broth.

3. Cover and cook on medium heat for 30 minutes. Reduce heat to low. Stir in potato and rosemary.

4. Serve with garlic bread croutons.

Yield: 6 to 8 servings

If you know where to look, the forest offers its own seasonal specialties: sorrel, spearmint, chickweed green briar tips, cinnamon vine, potato vine, poke sallet, wild garlic, lamb's quarters, violets, and sweet goldenrod. Don't eat any plant you can't positively identify.

Wild Sallet Soup

1. Melt butter in a skillet. Sauté potato until tender but not mushy. Add garlic when almost done sautéing.

2. Place sallet in a separate pan. Add enough water to cover. Bring to a boil. Drain.

3. Add sorrel and 2 quarts water. Bring to a boil. Reduce heat and simmer 10 minutes. Combine egg yolks with potato. Stir into soup. Add salt and remaining 5 ingredients.

4. Simmer 3 to 5 minutes. Serve hot.

Yield: 8 *servings*

4	tablespoons butter
½	cup wild potatoes, cubed
6	cloves wild garlic, minced
1	cup chopped young poke sallet
1	cup sorrel
2	quarts water
4	egg yolks, beaten
1	tablespoon salt
	Freshly ground black pepper to taste
1	teaspoon minced fresh sage
1	teaspoon minced fresh thyme
3	tablespoons chopped fresh parsley
¼	cup chopped fresh sweet goldenrod leaves

If you have difficulty finding any of the herbs found throughout the book, try calling the San Francisco Herb Company at 1-800-227-4530. Ask for a catalog.

Spring

Lamb's Quarter Salad

Poppy Seed Dressing

1	cup fruit juice of choice
½	cup honey
¼	cup basil vinegar
2	teaspoons poppy seed
1	teaspoon salt
6	cloves wild garlic, chopped

Salad

2	cups lamb's quarter
½	cup violet leaves and flowers
¼	cup chickweed tips
½	cup green briar tips
1	(11-ounce) can mandarin oranges, drained and chilled
¼	cup walnut pieces
¼	cup chopped spearmint

1. Process juice and next 5 ingredients in a blender; set aside.

2. To prepare salad, combine lamb's quarters and remaining 6 ingredients. Serve with poppy seed dressing.

Yield: 1¾ to 2 cups dressing, 4 salad servings

Barley Spring Salad

1. Cook barley in salted water. Cool.

2. Add green onions and remaining ingredients.

Yield: 4 to 6 servings

For a milder onion flavor in a salad, soak onions in a vinaigrette dressing for several hours before using. Drain onions and discard dressing.

1   cup barley
2   cups salted water
Green onions, chopped
Bell pepper or celery, chopped (optional)
Herb vinaigrette dressing
Fresh herbs of choice
Salt and pepper to taste

Marinated Pasta Shells

1. Combine oil and next 4 ingredients to make a marinade. Cook macaroni in lightly salted boiling water until tender but not overcooked.

2. Drain and immediately add marinade. Toss well to coat. Cover and refrigerate.

3. Before serving, bring macaroni to room temperature. Sprinkle with cheese and toss.

Yield: 4 servings

Modify dish by mixing leftovers with 1 to 2 cups cooked and halved pole beans. Marinate in refrigerator overnight before serving.

¼   cup oil
2   tablespoons chopped fresh basil, or 2 teaspoons dried
4   cloves garlic, finely minced
½   teaspoon crushed red pepper flakes
⅓   cup basil vinegar
8   ounces medium shell-shaped macaroni
½   cup grated Romano cheese

Spring

Tropical Slaw

½ cup white vinegar
⅓ cup sugar
¼ cup vegetable oil
¼ cup orange juice
2 (16-ounce) packages slaw mix
2 teaspoons salt
2 teaspoons black pepper
1 small onion, chopped
1 bell pepper, chopped
½ cup grated carrot
2 oranges, peeled and chopped
1 cup chopped fresh parsley

1. Shake together vinegar and next 3 ingredients in a jar. Refrigerate until chilled.

2. In a large bowl, combine dressing mixture with slaw mix and remaining ingredients.

3. Cover and refrigerate 1 hour to allow flavor to develop.

Yield: 20 servings

Herbal Gift Basket

Need a gift for the gardener? Purchase a basket and fill it with herb seed packages, herbed vinegar, this herb cookbook, and herbal soap. Tie top of basket with bunches of fresh herbs.

Sumi Salad

1. Break up noodles and discard seasoning packets. Combine noodles and cole slaw mix.

2. Roast almonds and sesame seeds in 1 teaspoon oil until browned. Add to cole slaw mixture.

3. Combine remaining 1 cup oil, sugar, and next 4 ingredients in a shaker bottle. Pour over cole slaw mixture.

4. Add rosemary and parsley, and mix well.

Yield: 8 to 10 servings

2 (3-ounce) packages dry ramen noodle soup
1 (16-ounce) package cole slaw mix
1 (2.25-ounce) package sliced or slivered almonds
½ cup sesame seeds
1 cup plus 1 teaspoon salad oil, divided
¼ cup sugar
1 teaspoon salt
1 teaspoon white pepper
2 teaspoons seasoned salt flavor enhancer
6 tablespoons rice vinegar
1 teaspoon fresh rosemary
1 tablespoon fresh minced parsley

Spring

Slaw With Chinese Noodles

1 (16-ounce) package cole slaw mix
4 green onions, diced
3 tablespoons vinegar
¼ cup oil
1 teaspoon salt
½ teaspoon black pepper
2 tablespoons sugar
1 teaspoon dried thyme
1 (3-ounce) package chicken-flavored dry ramen noodle soup
½ cup slivered almonds, toasted

1. Combine cole slaw mix and green onions; set aside.

2. Blend vinegar and next 5 ingredients. Mix in seasoning packet from soup. Pour mixture over cole slaw. and toss well.

3. Marinate at least 4 hours. Break up soup noodles. Add noodles and almonds to cole slaw just before serving.

Yield: 4 servings

To break noodles, place in a plastic bag and roll with a rolling pin.

Fresh sage can help sinus problems. Bruise a handful of fresh sage leaves, and add them to a small pan of water. Boil the water for 5 minutes; then breathe the steam to open up your head. This liquid can be refrigerated and reused many times.

Spinach Salad With Herbs

1. Clean spinach and remove broken stems. Tear into bite-size pieces. Place in a serving bowl and chill thoroughly.

2. Peel leaves from thyme sprigs and add to spinach. Chop chive blossoms and add to spinach, or leave whole and add to top of salad before serving.

3. Add cheese and onion rings just before adding dressing. Toss well.

4. To make dressing, mix soup and remaining 6 ingredients in a bowl. Whip with an electric mixer to thoroughly blend in oil. Pour over spinach mixture. Toss well.

Yield: 8 servings

Salad

- 1 bunch fresh spinach
- 8 sprigs fresh lemon thyme
- 8 fresh or frozen chive blossoms
- 2 tablespoons crumbled blue cheese
- 1 (2.8-ounce) can French-fried onion rings

Dressing

- ½ (10¾-ounce) can condensed tomato soup
- ¼ cup olive oil
- 6 tablespoons vinegar
- 6 tablespoons sugar
- ¼ teaspoon salt
- ½ teaspoon dry mustard
- ⅛ teaspoon paprika

Spring

Tarragon Chicken Salad

✓

Tarragon Dressing

⅓ cup tarragon wine vinegar

1 teaspoon chopped fresh tarragon

2 cloves garlic, halved

1 heaping teaspoon Dijon mustard

½ teaspoon paprika

½ cup extra virgin olive oil

Salad

1 (7-ounce) package vermicelli

6 chicken breasts

4 chicken bouillon cubes

1 tablespoon chopped fresh tarragon

1 (14-ounce) can artichoke hearts, drained and sliced

1 (6-ounce) can pitted black olives, drained and halved

3 green onions, thinly sliced

1-2 cups low fat mayonnaise

Salt and pepper

Sprigs of fresh parsley for garnish

1. Prepare dressing at least 2 days before serving by combining vinegar and next 4 ingredients. Mix well. Whip in oil. Refrigerate.

2. One day before serving, break vermicelli into thirds. Cook al dente in lightly salted water. Drain and immediately toss hot pasta with tarragon dressing. Discard garlic, cover, and refrigerate.

3. Prepare chicken also on day before serving. Cover chicken with cold water in a pot and bring to a boil. Turn off heat and let stand 1 minute. Drain and wash off scum; remove chicken skin, and return chicken to a clean pot.

4. Add enough water to just cover chicken. Add bouillon cubes and tarragon. Bring to a boil. Reduce heat, cover, and simmer 20 minutes. Turn off heat and let cool. Refrigerate chicken in broth overnight.

5. On day of serving, remove chicken from broth and debone. Cut meat into bite-size pieces. Combine chicken, pasta, artichoke, olives, and green onions. Mix in mayonnaise. Season with salt and pepper. Garnish.

Yield: 10 to 12 servings

Artichokes and olives tossed in a flavor-laden dressing result in a very delicious salad.

Pasta Salad

1. Cook macaroni according to package. Drain.

2. Cut vegetables into bite-size pieces. Add vegetables to macaroni.

3. Combine oil, vinegar, and sugar. Pour over macaroni mixture and toss.

4. Add herbs, salt, and pepper. Mix well. Marinate overnight.

Yield: 4 to 6 servings

Because this salad marinates overnight, it is not a good idea to use onions. Fresh herbs such as oregano, thyme, parsley, marjoram, and basil work well.

1   (8-ounce) package macaroni
Vegetables of choice
1   cup olive oil
1   cup vinegar
1   cup sugar
Chopped fresh herbs of choice
Salt and pepper to taste

Strawberry-Chicken Salad

1. Divide greens evenly between 4 plates. Sprinkle with celery. Chill until serving time.

2. Cut chicken into bite-size strips. Combine chicken and vinaigrette in a bowl. Marinate in refrigerator for at least 60 minutes, longer if possible. Drain, discarding marinade.

3. Sauté chicken over medium-high heat until thoroughly cooked and lightly browned. Divide chicken among plates of greens.

4. Deglaze sauté pan with 1 to 2 tablespoons of poppy seed dressing. Pour over chicken. Distribute strawberries on salads. Pour poppy seed dressing over top.

Yield: 4 servings

4   cups assorted greens
½   cup sliced celery
1   pound raw chicken (meat only)
½   cup tarragon or raspberry vinaigrette
8   fresh strawberries, sliced
½   cup poppy seed dressing

Side Dishes

Herb-Stuffed Mushrooms

30	mushrooms
1¼	cups red wine, divided
1	onion, chopped
2	large cloves garlic
3	tablespoons fresh basil
1	tablespoon fresh thyme
	Butter for sautéing
1½	cups Italian-style breadcrumbs
3	tablespoons soy sauce, divided
	Parmesan cheese to taste

1. Hollow out mushrooms; set aside.

2. Combine 1 to 2 tablespoons wine and next 4 ingredients in a food processor. Sauté mixture in butter. Mix in breadcrumbs, 2 tablespoons soy sauce, ¼ cup wine, and cheese. Add water if mixture is too stiff.

3. Place mixture in a pastry bag and pipe into mushrooms. Place mushrooms in a jellyroll pan. Pour remaining wine and soy sauce into pan. Cover with foil.

4. Bake at 325° for 10 to 20 minutes or until tender.

Yield: 8 to 10 side-dish servings or 16 to 20 appetizer servings

Bath bags: Place a mixture of oatmeal, marjoram, lemon balm, chamomile, and pennyroyal into inexpensive washcloths. Tie with a long ribbon, and hang on faucet in tub. Let warm water run through the bag, and use to rub on aching muscles.

Green Sugar Snap Peas With Tarragon

1. Cook peas in salted water for 4 to 5 minutes or until crisp-tender. Drain.

2. Add butter and remaining ingredients. Mix well to coat peas.

Yield: 4 servings

¾ cup sugar snap peas, trimmed
2 tablespoons butter
2 teaspoon chopped fresh tarragon or parsley
⅛ teaspoon ground cumin
Salt and freshly ground pepper

Cheese Grits With Mint

1. Combine egg with enough milk to equal 1 cup. Combine egg mixture with water and next 3 ingredients. Mix well.

2. Pour mixture into a greased casserole dish. Top with Cheddar cheese, mint, and paprika.

3. Bake at 350° for 45 minutes. Serve warm or at room temperature.

Yield: 4 servings

Serve this dish at a breakfast buffet with a bowl of fresh fruit and a basket of sausage biscuits.

1 egg
Milk
3 cups water
1 cup grits
1 stick butter or margarine, softened
1 (6-ounce) garlic cheese link
Grated Cheddar cheese
Chopped fresh mint
Paprika

Spring

Mexican Black-eyed Peas

1 (16-ounce) package dried black-eyed peas
2 pounds bulk pork sausage
1 medium onion, finely chopped
1 (28-ounce) can whole tomatoes, undrained
½ cup water
2 tablespoons sugar
1½-2½ tablespoons chili powder
2½ tablespoons finely chopped celery
2 teaspoons garlic salt
¼ teaspoon black pepper
1 teaspoon dried oregano

1. Wash and sort peas. Place peas in a large Dutch oven and add enough water to cover 2 inches above top of peas. Soak overnight.

2. Brown sausage in a heavy skillet, stirring to crumble. Add onion and cook until tender. Drain sausage.

3. Drain peas well. Stir in sausage, tomatoes and remaining 7 ingredients. Bring to a boil. Reduce heat and cover. Simmer 1 hour, 30 minutes, adding water if necessary.

Yield: 10 servings

Dilly Carrots

1 pound carrots, peeled and julienne
½ cup water
¼ cup cider vinegar
1 teaspoon dried French tarragon, crushed
1 teaspoon dried dill
1 teaspoon sugar

 1. Place all ingredients in a medium saucepan. Bring to a boil. Cover and reduce heat.

2. Simmer 30 minutes or until crisp-tender. Chill overnight. Drain before serving.

Yield: 4 to 6 servings

Candied Carrots With Fresh Herbs

1. Slice carrots lengthwise and then in half. Melt butter in a large saucepan. Add broth. Spread carrot slices evenly throughout pan. Cook over medium heat until tender.

2. Remove carrot slices to a serving dish and keep warm, leaving sauce in pan.

3. Cook sauce over medium to medium-high heat until reduced to ¼ cup. Monitor closely to prevent burning sauce. Pour sauce over slices.

4. Sprinkle with salt, pepper, and remaining 3 ingredients.

Yield: 8 to 10 servings

1½ pounds fresh carrots
2 sticks butter or margarine
2 cups chicken broth
Salt and pepper to taste
1½ teaspoons finely chopped fresh lemon verbena
1½ teaspoons finely chopped fresh basil
1 teaspoon finely chopped fresh thyme

Raspberry Thyme Carrots

1. Cook carrots 4 to 6 minutes or until crisp-tender. Do not overcook. Drain well.

2. While carrots are still warm, add vinegar. Mix in oil, lemon thyme, and black pepper.

3. Serve immediately or marinate in refrigerator overnight.

Yield: 4 to 6 servings

If marinating overnight, remove from refrigerator 1 hour before serving.

1 pound carrots, peeled and sliced
½ cup raspberry vinegar
½ cup virgin olive oil
3 tablespoons fresh lemon thyme
Freshly ground black pepper to taste

Spring

Eggplant With Herbs

3   eggplants
3   large Bermuda
    onions
Oil for sautéing
3   tablespoons finely
    chopped fresh
    parsley
½   teaspoon dried
    sweet basil
1   teaspoon dried
    rosemary
½   teaspoon salt
½   teaspoon black
    pepper
2   tablespoons butter
1   cup breadcrumbs

1. Peel eggplants and cut into ¾-inch cubes. Boil in salted water for 5 minutes. Drain.

2. Slice onions and separate into rings. Sauté onion in oil for 3 to 4 minutes without browning.

3. In a separate bowl, combine parsley and next 4 ingredients.

4. In a greased casserole dish, alternate layers of eggplant and onion. Dot each eggplant layer with butter and sprinkle with seasoning mixture. Top final layer with breadcrumbs and dot with butter.

5. Bake uncovered at 375° for 30 minutes.

Yield: 8 servings

Herb-baked Potatoes

2   medium to large
    baking potatoes
1   stick butter,
    melted
2   tablespoons
    chopped fresh
    parsley
1   tablespoon
    chopped fresh
    basil
1   tablespoon
    chopped fresh
    chives

1. Clean potatoes thoroughly. Place a wooden spoon handle behind potato to prevent slicing through whole potato. Cut ¼-inch slices into potatoes, keeping bottom of slices attached. Place in ice water for 30 minutes. Remove from water and dry thoroughly.

2. Combine butter and remaining 3 ingredients. Carefully separate slices and baste all surfaces with butter mixture.

3. Microwave on high for 8 to 9 minutes.

Yield: 2 servings

Rosemary Potatoes

 1. Combine oil, garlic, and rosemary. Pour over potatoes and toss to evenly coat.

2. Place in a microwave-safe dish. Cover with plastic wrap and puncture with 2 holes for ventilation.

3. Microwave on medium to high for 12 minutes. Check potatoes.

4. When potatoes are soft, remove plastic wrap and place dish under broiler. Cook until potatoes brown. Toss and continue to broil to further brown potatoes. Season with salt and pepper.

Yield: 6 to 8 servings

1 tablespoon olive oil
1 tablespoon chopped garlic
1 tablespoon chopped fresh rosemary
4 large red potatoes, thinly sliced
Salt and pepper to taste

Sautéed Herbed Rice

1. Coat a heavy skillet with nonstick cooking spray. Add oil and heat over medium heat. Add rice and onion. Sauté until rice is lightly browned.

2. Stir in broth and remaining 4 ingredients. Bring to a boil. Cover and reduce heat. Simmer 20 to 25 minutes or until rice is tender and water is absorbed.

Yield: 7 servings

1 teaspoon olive oil
1 cup uncooked rice
½ cup chopped onion
1 (14½-ounce) can chicken broth
¼ cup water
1 teaspoon whole dried rosemary
½ teaspoon whole dried marjoram
½ teaspoon whole dried savory

Spring

Microwaved Pipérade

1 medium onion, minced

1 small bell pepper, seeded and finely chopped

1 small red bell pepper, seeded and finely chopped

2 tablespoons olive or vegetable oil

2 medium-size ripe tomatoes, peeled, seeded, and coarsely chopped

1 clove garlic, crushed

1 teaspoon minced fresh basil, or ¼ teaspoon dried

½ teaspoon salt

⅛ teaspoon black pepper

3 ounces ham, cut in strips

2 tablespoons butter or margarine

6 eggs, lightly beaten

1. In a shallow 9-inch microwave casserole dish, combine onion, bell peppers, and oil. Cover with wax paper and microwave on high power for 6 minutes, stirring once half-way through cooking.

2. Add tomatoes and garlic and microwave uncovered on high power for 2 minutes. Stir. Continue cooking for 3 minutes or until most of liquid evaporates. If tomatoes are very juicy, drain excess liquid at this time.

3. Mix in basil and next 3 ingredients. Cover with foil. Place butter in an 8-inch round glass dish. Cover with wax paper and micro-wave on high power for 35 to 45 seconds or until melted. Tilt dish to coat sides.

4. Add egg and microwave uncovered on high power for 2 minutes. Draw partially cooked edges toward center. Cook another 1½ to 2 minutes or until egg just sets.

5. Sprinkle vegetable mixture evenly over the top. Cut into wedges.

Yield: 4 servings

Not a quiche, not an omelet, but a Basque egg dish based on tomatoes and peppers.

Fettuccine Alfredo With Herbs

 1. Cook fettuccine according to package directions; drain.

2. Melt butter in a large pan. Stir in cheese and half-and-half. Bring to a simmer. Add parsley and next 3 ingredients. Mix in fettuccine and meat.

Yield: 4 servings

8	ounces fettuccine
4	tablespoons butter
½	cup Parmesan cheese
1	cup half-and-half
1½	tablespoons dried parsley
1½	tablespoons dried basil
1½	tablespoons dried thyme
1½	tablespoons dried marjoram
	Cooked chicken, shrimp, crabmeat, or lobster (optional)

Poached Salmon

1. Combine wine and next 6 ingredients in a large skillet. Bring to a boil. Cover and reduce heat. Simmer 10 minutes.

2. Add salmon. Cover and simmer 8 minutes or until salmon flakes easily with a fork.

Yield: 4 servings

Russian and Scandinavian cooks have long known the secret of dill with fresh salmon.

1½	cups dry white wine or cooking wine
½	cup water
1	onion, sliced
1	lemon, sliced
4	sprigs fresh parsley
1	teaspoon dried dill
¼	teaspoon black pepper
4	salmon steaks (about 1½ pounds)

Spring

Low Fat Chicken-in-a-Pot

8 new potatoes, halved
4 carrots, cut in 2 pieces
4 chicken breasts, skinned
⅛ teaspoon garlic powder
1 teaspoon curry powder
½ teaspoon dry mustard
1 teaspoon dried tarragon
2 tablespoons lemon juice
½ cup white wine
4 stalks celery, thinly sliced
4 onion, thinly sliced

 1. Combine potato and carrot in a casserole dish. Place chicken on top.

2. Mix together garlic powder and next 5 ingredients. Pour over chicken. Top with celery and onion.

3. Cover and bake at 350° for 60 minutes or until vegetables are tender.

Yield: 4 servings

A splendid blend of herbs to make the most of chicken, new potatoes, and your low-fat intentions.

Chicken and Asparagus With Sweet Marjoram

 1. Cut asparagus into 1½-inch pieces. Steam until crisp-tender.

2. Coat a sauté pan with nonstick cooking spray. Lightly brown chicken on both sides. Place chicken in a single layer in a greased baking pan. Sprinkle with sweet marjoram. Arrange asparagus on top.

3. Add margarine to sauté pan. Sauté onion and garlic until tender. Sprinkle with flour and brown for 1 minute. Add broth and cook and stir until sauce thickens.

4. Add wine and mushrooms and simmer 2 minutes. Taste for proper seasoning, adding salt and pepper as needed. Pour sauce over chicken.

5. Bake at 350° for 30 minutes or until done. Garnish.

Yield: 6 servings

One sure sign of spring is the day the asparagus pushes through the ground and bunches of the tender vegetable are at the grocery store.

1 pound fresh asparagus
6 chicken breasts, boned and skinned
3 tablespoons chopped fresh sweet marjoram
1 tablespoon margarine
½ cup chopped onion
1 large clove garlic
2 tablespoons all-purpose flour
1½ cups low-fat chicken broth
½ cup dry white wine
1 (4-ounce) can mushroom slices or stems and pieces, drained
Salt and pepper to taste
Sprigs of fresh sweet marjoram for garnish

Marjoram was used to brew ale before hops were introduced.

Chicken Breasts With Low-Fat Pesto

4 chicken breasts, boned and skinned
2/3 cup tightly packed fresh basil leaves
1 clove garlic
1 tablespoon Parmesan cheese
1/8 teaspoon black pepper
1/4 cup fat-free yogurt

1. Heat a stainless-steel skillet coated with nonstick cooking spray over high heat. Add chicken and quickly brown on both sides.

2. Place chicken in a microwave-safe baking dish. Process basil and next 3 ingredients in a food processor until finely chopped. Add yogurt and blend until smooth.

3. Spread pesto mixture over chicken. Cover loosely with wax paper. Heat in microwave at 70% power for 7 to 10 minutes or until chicken is tender.

Yield: 4 servings

Italian Gift Basket

Use container from beer or wine coolers; spray paint white and decorate. Add 1 bottle wine, 1 small loaf bread, 1 can spaghetti sauce, and spaghetti.

Breast Of Chicken Parisienne

1. Melt butter in a sauté pan. Add chicken and brown on both sides.

2. Remove chicken. Add chives, mushrooms, and lemon juice to pan. Season with salt and pepper. Cook for 3 minutes.

3. Return chicken to pan. Add wine and rosemary. Cover and simmer 20 minutes or until chicken is tender.

4. Combine yogurt and flour. Stir into pan juices and cook 3 minutes. Serve chicken on rice with sauce spooned over the top. Garnish.

Yield: *4 servings*

6 tablespoons butter
4 chicken breasts, boned and skinned
2 tablespoons chopped fresh chives
8 ounces fresh mushrooms, sliced
1 tablespoon lemon juice
Salt and pepper
½ cup dry white wine
½ teaspoon dried rosemary
1 cup plain yogurt, low fat, if desired
1 tablespoon all-purpose flour
Cooked rice
Sprigs of fresh parsley for garnish

Spring

Chicken Niçoise

1 teaspoon olive oil
4 chicken breasts, boned and skinned
Salt and pepper to taste
½ cup finely chopped onion
2 large cloves garlic, pressed
3 medium to large tomatoes, diced
1½ teaspoons herbes de Provence
½ cup dry white wine
25 Niçoise olives
Cooked rice

1. Coat a sauté pan with nonstick cooking spray. Add oil and heat pan. Add chicken and quickly brown on both sides. Sprinkle with salt and pepper. Remove chicken from pan.

2. Combine onion and garlic in pan and cook over low heat until tender. Add tomato, herbes de Provence, and extra salt. Cover and simmer about 5 minutes.

3. Return chicken to pan, spooning vegetables over chicken. Add wine and olives. Cover and simmer 20 minutes or until chicken is tender. Stir occasionally. Remove cover for last 5 minutes of cooking to allow sauce to thicken. Taste for proper seasoning.

4. Serve chicken and sauce with rice.

Yield: 4 servings

 The Romans wore parsley garlands around their necks to absorb fumes from wine.

Brandied Ham

1. Score fat on ham. Combine brown sugar and maple syrup to make a paste. Spread paste over ham. Stick cloves in surface of ham. Fasten bay leaves to ham using tooth-picks.

2. Place ham in a pan. Pour brandy in pan and cover.

3. Bake at 450° for 20 minutes per pound of ham. After 10 minutes in oven, add water. During last hour of cooking time, baste frequently with pan juices.

4. Refrigerate overnight to allow surface to glaze.

Yield: *16 to 20 servings*

With its garland of bay leaves, this ham is an Olympian treat. It may be a good choice for Easter dinner.

1	(8- to 10-pound) boiled ham, skin and rind removed
1	cup packed brown sugar
1	cup maple syrup or honey
	Whole cloves
12	dried bay leaves
2	cups brandy
2	cups water

Spring

Italian Casserole

1   pound ground beef or turkey
½   teaspoon Italian seasoning
1   (16-ounce) jar spaghetti sauce
1   cup uncooked elbow macaroni or small shells
1   cup water
½-¾   cup grated mozzarella cheese

1. Place beef in a 10x7x2-inch microwave-safe casserole dish. Cook in a microwave oven on high power 4 to 6 minutes or until browned. Stir occasionally while cooking. Drain.

2. Combine Italian seasoning and sauce. Add sauce, macaroni, and water to beef. Mix well.

3. Cover and cook on high power for 13 minutes or until macaroni is tender. Stir once half-way through cooking time.

4. Top with cheese and cook on high for 2 minutes or until cheese melts.

Yield: 4 servings

Provençal Leg Of Lamb

1   (5-pound) leg of lamb
4   cloves garlic, quartered
1   handful sprigs of fresh rosemary

1. Wash leg of lamb and pat dry. Cut 12 to 16 small slits on the upper surface. In each slit, place a piece of garlic and about 3 rosemary leaves. Use a small knife, if necessary, to push garlic and rosemary under the skin.

2. Place on a roasting rack. Bake at 350° for 2 hours.

Yield: 8 to 10 servings

This very simple recipe results in a deliciously tender, rosemary-infused roast.

Desserts

Chocolate Mint Pie

1. Melt chocolate chips in a double boiler.

2. Mix chocolate with egg and next 4 ingredients in a large bowl. Add flour and chopped mint. Mix well.

3. Divide evenly into pie shells. Bake at 350° for 30 minutes.

4. Serve with a dollop of whipped cream and garnish.

Yield: 16 servings

2 cups chocolate chips
4 eggs, slightly beaten
2 cups sugar
2 sticks butter, melted
2 teaspoons vanilla
2 cups chopped pecans or walnuts
1 cup all-purpose flour
1 tablespoon finely chopped fresh chocolate mint
2 (9-inch) pie shells, unbaked
Sprigs of fresh chocolate mint for garnish

In the Middle Ages if rosemary thrived in a garden, the woman was said to rule the home. And, it was favored for sweetening the breath as well as lifting the spirits.

Spring

Pineapple Dream Torte

1 teaspoon vinegar
1½ teaspoons vanilla
8 egg whites, room temperature
2 cups sugar
1 cup crushed and drained pineapple
½ cup chopped and drained maraschino cherries
2 cups whipped cream
2 tablespoons chopped fresh pineapple sage leaves
Fresh pineapple sage blossoms for garnish

1. To make meringue, add vinegar and vanilla to egg whites and beat until mixture forms peaks. Add sugar slowly and beat until stiff.

2. Line two 9-inch cake pans with brown paper. Spread mixture into pans. Bake at 300° for 1 hour, 15 minutes. Cool before removing from pans.

3. Fold pineapple and cherries into whipped cream. Spread half of mixture on one layer of meringue. Cover with second meringue layer. Frost with remainder of cream mixture. Chill overnight.

4. Sprinkle pineapple sage leaves over top. Garnish on top and around sides of torte.

Yield: 8 to 10 servings

Cinnamon Stick Basket

Cut cinnamon sticks into 4-inch pieces, and glue together to form a square for the sides of the basket. Keep adding sticks to make the bottom of the basket. Then make a square U-shaped handle out of the sticks, and glue to top. Decorate with dried roses. Let dry overnight.

Sally G's Strawberries

1. Place strawberries in a bowl. Pour lemonade concentrate over strawberries. Add citrus mint and mix well. Refrigerate several hours.

2. Serve in sherbet glasses topped with whipped cream and sprigs of mint.

Yield: 4 to 6 servings

File this unusual dessert combination under fast.

1 quart strawberries, cleaned and sliced
1 (6-ounce) can frozen pink lemonade concentrate, thawed
1 tablespoon chopped fresh citrus mint
Whipped cream and sprigs of fresh citrus mint for garnish

Cinnamon Topsy

1. Melt 2 tablespoons butter. Cream with sugar. Mix in egg and cinnamon basil.

2. Sift together flour and baking powder. Add dry ingredients and milk alternately to creamed mixture.

3. Spread evenly in a 11x7x2-inch pan. Cover with brown sugar. Dot with remaining 4 tablespoons butter. Sprinkle generously with cinnamon.

4. Bake at 425° for 25 to 30 minutes.

Yield: 6 to 8 servings

It's a cross between muffins, shortcake, and cookies. This dessert is a treat with a cup of tea or a glass of milk, or a good dessert for picnics.

6 tablespoons butter or margarine, divided
1½ cups sugar
1 egg
½ cup chopped fresh cinnamon basil
2 cups all-purpose flour
2 teaspoons baking powder
1 cup milk
1 cup packed light brown sugar
Cinnamon for topping

Spring

Jim Cardell's New York Cheesecake

1   (16-ounce) container cottage cheese
2   (8-ounce) packages cream cheese
1½ cups sugar
4   eggs
Juice of 1 lemon
3   tablespoons all-purpose flour
3   tablespoons cornstarch
1   stick butter, melted
2   cups sour cream
1½ tablespoons vanilla
¼   cup finely chopped fresh lemon verbena

1. Combine ingredients in order listed, beating with an electric mixer for 1½ minutes after each addition. Pour batter into a well-greased 9- or 10-inch springform pan.

2. Bake at 325° for 60 minutes or until center is firm. Allow to cool 2 hours in oven. Chill. Serve in wedges.

Yield: 12 servings

Sleep Pillow: Fill a soft muslin bag with dried flowers of chamomile, lavender, marjoram, and catnip. Place beside your bed pillow to give rest and sweet dreams.

Lemon Verbena Almond Wafers ✓

1. Cream butter and sugar with an electric mixer until fluffy. Beat in egg. Beat in vanilla.

2. Gradually mix in flour until blended. Stir in lemon zest and lemon verbena.

3. Drop by heaping half teaspoons, 2 inches apart, onto an ungreased baking sheet. Gently press a few almond slices into center of each cookie.

4. Bake at 350° for 8 to 10 minutes or until edges are golden brown. Let cool on sheet on a rack for 1 to 2 minutes. Carefully remove from sheet and place directly on rack to cool completely.

Yield: 4 to 5 dozen

These cookies are very tender. If cooled too long on baking sheet, they will break when trying to remove them. If this happens, return cookies to oven for about 1 minute before trying again.

2   sticks butter, softened
1   cup sugar
1   egg
1   teaspoon vanilla
2   cups cake flour
1½ tablespoons lemon zest
2   tablespoons chopped dried lemon verbena or 3 tablespoons fresh
Sliced almonds for garnish

Lavender Cookies

½	cup shortening
1	stick butter or margarine, softened
2	eggs
1⅓	cups granulated sugar
⅓	cup packed brown sugar
3½	cups all-purpose flour
¼	teaspoon salt
1	teaspoon baking soda
1	teaspoon cream of tartar
3-5	tablespoons dried lavender
1½	teaspoons vanilla

1. Blend shortening and next 4 ingredients. Combine flour and next 3 ingredients. Add dry ingredient mixture to shortening mixture. Mix well. Blend in lavender and vanilla.

2. Divide dough into thirds and shape into rolls. Wrap in wax paper and refrigerate about 6 hours or overnight. Cut slices a little less than ¼ inch thick. Place on an ungreased baking sheet, allowing room in-between for cookies to spread.

3. Bake at 350° for 5 to 7 minutes or until cookies begin to change color.

Yield: 6 to 7 dozen cookies

Whirling lavender in a food processor before using helps to bring out flavor.

 Press herbs between the sheets of an old telephone book to preserve them.

Lemon Thins

Cookies

1½	cups all-purpose flour
½	teaspoon baking soda
½	teaspoon salt
½	cup shortening
¾	cup sugar
1	egg
1	tablespoon lemon juice
2	teaspoons lemon zest
1-2	tablespoons minced fresh lemon verbena

Lemon Glaze (optional)

2	tablespoons lemon juice
1	cup powdered sugar
1	teaspoon butter, softened

1. Stir together flour, baking soda, and salt. In a separate bowl, cream shortening and sugar. Beat in egg and next 3 ingredients. Stir in dry ingredients thoroughly.

2. Shape dough into two 6-inch rolls. Wrap tightly with wax paper or plastic wrap. Freeze overnight.

3. When ready to bake cookies, slice dough slightly thicker than ⅛-inch. Place cookies 1 inch apart on an ungreased baking sheet.

4. Bake at 375° for 8 to 10 minutes or until edges are golden. Remove from baking sheet and place on a cooling rack.

5. To make lemon glaze, combine lemon juice, sugar, and butter. Frost cookies with glaze.

Yield: about 3 dozen

Steep lemon verbena leaves in hot lemon juice to intensify juice's flavor.

Spring

Lemon Balm Cookies

1½ sticks butter, softened

1 (3-ounce) package cream cheese, softened

1 tablespoon baking powder

½ teaspoon salt

1 cup sugar

1 egg, room temperature

1 tablespoon fresh lemon juice

3 tablespoons finely chopped fresh lemon balm

3 cups all-purpose flour

1. Cream butter and cream cheese until fluffy. Blend in baking powder and next 5 ingredients. Gradually mix in flour. Add more flour if necessary to knead into a soft dough.

2. Fit a cookie press with a template that forms a strip of dough flat on the bottom and ridged on the top. Force dough through press directly onto a baking sheet to form wavy-shaped cookies 3 to 4 inches long.

3. Bake at 375° for 7 to 10 minutes or until slightly brown around the edges. Cool on a rack.

Yield: 6 dozen cookies

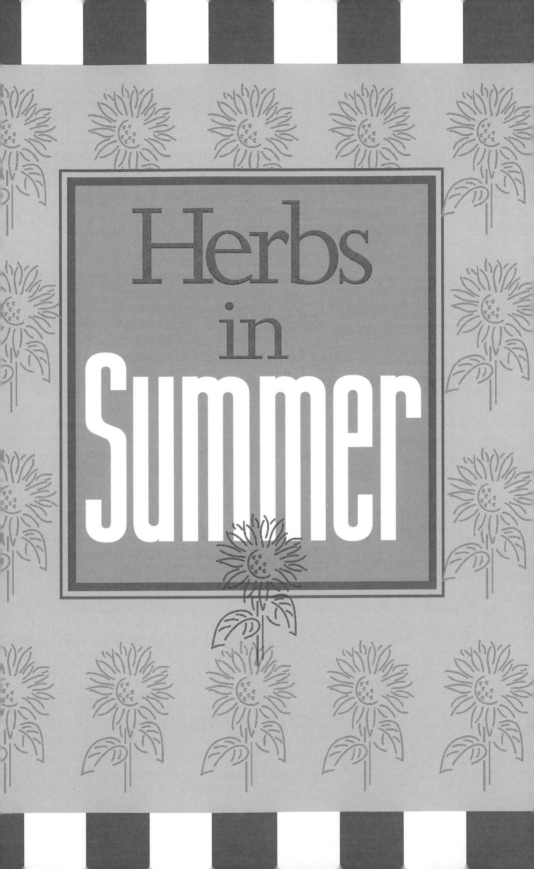

Herbs in Summer

The season could as well be called, "abundance." Gardens and markets offer fresh herbs, ready for matching with all the favorite fresh fruits and vegetables. The herb enthusiast has plenty of opportunities to use herbs creatively. Herbs make the whole season one of celebration.

Herbs in Summer

Take time to smell the basil when its scent lingers after a summer thunderstorm.

Herbs are linked with wedding and romance legends. Traditionally, bridesmaids tucked a sprig of lavender next to the groom's boutonniere as a symbol of fidelity. Young lovers were crowned with garlands of sweet marjoram in ancient Greece and Rome.

Offer a bouquet of scented herbs — rosemary, scented geraniums, lemon verbena, lemon thyme, mint, sage, and basil — as a hostess gift.

Use herbs for pest control. Summer campers are said to benefit from pungent garlic in their diets to help keep mosquitoes away. Mint and pennyroyal are nature's own method of flea control. Mint's name itself is linked with the Greek for "flea." Grow a potful of these herbs at the doorstep to discourage the pests.

Herbs for Summer Weddings

June is still the month when many people get married. You can make that special occasion especially memorable with these herbal touches to the rehearsal dinner.

Rehearsal Dinner Favors: Tie one sprig of each of the following into a small bunch. Use a small or narrow ribbon for the groom and a wider ribbon for the bride. Present them with a small card listing the herbs and their meaning for the memory book. Suggest that they may dry the bunches to keep with the card.

Rehearsal Dinner Guest Favors: Present a sprig of rosemary for "remembrance" to each guest. Tie the sprig with a small ribbon in wedding colors and a card stating the meaning of the traditional wedding herb.

Groom's Favor	
wheat	prosperity
parsley	festivity
mint	virtue
thyme	strength
marjoram	joy
rose (tiny)	love
sage	health

Bride's Favor	
rose geranium	"My Beloved"
lavender	devotion
rosemary	remembrance
ivy	marriage
rue	grace or virginity
rose	love
feverfew blossom	"you light up my life"

Recipes for Rehearsal Dinner

Fogg Road Handful Tea

3   family-size tea
    bags
1   handful each of
    pineapple mint,
    spearmint, orange
    mint, chocolate
    mint
2   large handfuls
    pineapple sage
    leaves
4   large handfuls
    lemon balm
1   gallon water
Juice of 1 lemon
Sugar or low-calorie
    sweetener to taste

Wash all herbs. Place into a glass pot. Add
water, and bring to a boil. Remove from heat;
add lemon juice and sweetener while still hot.
Cover and steep for 3 hours. Chill until very
cold before serving.

Yield: 16 (1-cup) servings

This is a refreshing cold punch for a hot June day.

Garden Salad

Garden leaf lettuce,
    torn
Arugula, torn
Chives, chopped
Lovage leaves, torn
Opal basil, chopped
Salad burnet, torn
Red onion rings
Nasturtium blossoms

Toss together first 6 ingredients. Garnish with
onion rings and nasturtium blossoms. Serve
with Lemon Basil Salad Dressing.

Rehearsal Dinner

Lemon Basil Salad Dressing

Combine all ingredients in food processor or blender; process until smooth. Pour into a pitcher or bottle, cover, and refrigerate.

Yield: 5 to 6 cups

4 cups lemon basil, loosely packed
6 teaspoons fresh oregano leaves
1 cup fresh lemon juice
1 teaspoon salt
8 cloves garlic, peeled and minced
3 cups extra-virgin olive oil
2 cups Parmesan cheese
1 teaspoon coarsely ground pepper

Three-Herb Parmesan Chicken

Melt butter; stir in herbs. Coat chicken breasts with butter mixture. Bake, covered, at 350° for 45 to 60 minutes. Remove from oven; cover each breast with cheese and pepper. Return to oven, and broil, uncovered, to lightly brown.

Yield: 12 servings

3 sticks butter
3 teaspoons fresh marjoram
3 teaspoons lemon thyme
3 teaspoons sage
12 boneless chicken breasts, skinned
Parmesan cheese to taste
Black pepper to taste

Herbed Yogurt Dip

2 tablespoons
   chopped fresh
   chives or green
   onion stems
2 tablespoons
   chopped fresh
   parsley
1 tablespoon
   chopped fresh
   tarragon, dill, or
   Mexican mint
   marigold
1 clove garlic
1 (8-ounce)
   container plain
   low-fat yogurt
¼ cup low-fat or
   regular
   mayonnaise
Salt and pepper to
   taste

1. Process chives and next 3 ingredients in a blender or a food processor to a paste-like consistency. Add yogurt and mayonnaise. Stir with a rubber spatula to blend well. Season with salt and pepper.

2. Transfer to a small bowl, and refrigerate several hours.

Yield: 1¼ cups

Remove old flowers and leaves from lavender stems. Tie stems together with a ribbon. Use stems to scent linens drawers or shelves and other closets. Or place under pillows in the guestroom.

Eggplant Caviar

1. Wash eggplant and cut off stem. Bake eggplant on a baking sheet at 325° for 60 minutes. Cool eggplant for 30 minutes; then peel.

2. Finely chop together eggplant, onion, and tomatoes. Soak bread in vinegar. Add bread, thyme, and remaining 7 ingredients to vegetables. Continue chopping until well blended. Add more seasoning, as needed, to achieve a spicy flavor.

3. Serve with pumpernickel bread.

Yield: 10 to 12 servings

1	large eggplant
1	small onion, sliced
2	tomatoes, peeled
1	slice white bread, crust trimmed
3	tablespoons vinegar
	Pinch of dried thyme
	Pinch of dried basil
	Pinch of dried summer savory
	Pinch of dried fennel
1½	teaspoons salt
½	teaspoon black pepper
2	teaspoon sugar
4	tablespoons oil

Guacamole

1. Peel avocados and mash with a fork. Mix in garlic, lemon juice, and cilantro.

2. Spread mayonnaise on top to prevent darkening. Stir together just before serving.

Yield: about 1½ cups

2	very ripe large avocados
4	cloves garlic, minced
	Juice of 2 lemons
1	tablespoon chopped fresh cilantro
½	cup mayonnaise

Summer

Monterey Jack Cheese Dip

6 ounces Monterey Jack cheese, grated
1 (4½-ounce) can chopped green chiles
1 (2¼-ounce) can sliced or (4½-ounce) can diced black olives
6 green onions, chopped
3 tomatoes, seeded and chopped
¾ cup Italian dressing
¼ cup chopped fresh cilantro, or to taste

 1. Combine all ingredients. Chill well.

2. Serve with chips.

Yield: about 1 cup

Herbal Dip

¼ teaspoon fresh fennel
¼ teaspoon fresh dill
¼ teaspoon fresh mint
¼ teaspoon fresh cilantro
1 cup fat free cottage cheese
⅓ cup plain yogurt
2 tablespoons lemon juice
1 green onion, coarsely chopped
Salt and pepper to taste

1. Blend fennel and next 6 ingredients until smooth. Mix in green onion, salt, and pepper.

2. Serve with fresh vegetables, chips, or crackers.

Yield: 1¼ cups

Summer

Cucumber Spread With Lemon Thyme

1. Grind cucumber to a pulp in a blender or a food processor. Place on a double layer of cheesecloth and squeeze out juice.

2. Grind onion in blender or food processor. Add cucumber, cream cheese, and remaining 4 ingredients. Blend until fairly smooth. Refrigerate overnight.

3. Serve with fresh vegetables or crackers.

Yield: about 1 cup

1 medium cucumber, peeled and seeded
½ medium onion
1 (8-ounce) package cream cheese, softened
Dash of salt
Dash of hot pepper sauce
1 drop green food coloring (optional)
1 tablespoon fresh lemon thyme, or to taste

Spanish Deviled Eggs

1. Cut eggs in half lengthwise. Remove yolks. Mix yolks well in a bowl.

2. Add mayonnaise and next 5 ingredients.

3. Fill egg whites with mixture. Garnish.

Yield: 24 halves

12 hard boiled eggs
¼ cup mayonnaise
1 tablespoon sour cream
½ cup grated sharp cheddar cheese
¼ cup spicy salsa
2 tablespoons chopped fresh chives
Dash of cumin
Olive slices and sprigs of fresh cilantro for garnish

Victorian Party Sandwiches

2 sticks butter, softened

½ cup gourmet jam

2 tablespoons powdered milk

¼ cup fresh rosemary leaves, plus extra for garnish

¼ cup fresh lavender flower, plus extra for garnish

¼ cup fresh, unsprayed, and fragrant rose petals, plus extra for garnish

20 white bread slices, crusts removed

1. Combine butter and next 5 ingredients. Spread on bread slices. Cut each slice into 4 triangles. Sprinkle with rosemary, lavender, and rose petals reserved for garnish.

Yield: 16 to 20 appetizer servings

Freeze bread slices before cutting off crusts to prevent crushing.

Sample the leisure of a Victorian afternoon of long ago with an up-to-date set of sandwiches to serve with your favorite hot tea.

Tussie Mussies

Herbs and flowers from your garden
Rubberband
Wet cotton balls
Aluminum foil
Green florists tape
Ribbon
Lace tussie mussie holders
Straight pins

1. Gather a bunch of herbs and flowers the night before you make the tussie mussie. Put herbs and flowers in warm water overnight.
2. Bunch herbs and flowers around one perfect rose. Secure with rubberband.
3. Wrap wet cotton balls around ends of stems. Put foil around stems and cotton balls to hold moisture in. Wrap floral tape all over to hide foil. Then wrap with ribbon.
4. Make a bow with additional ribbon; set aside. Put herb and flower stems into tussie mussie holder. Wrap tape around stems and tussie mussie holder to secure them together. Add more ribbon to top. Pin on bow.

Orange Mint Jelly

1. Combine mint and orange juice in a saucepan. Bring to a boil. Turn off heat, cover, and cool. Strain juice.

2. Measure 3 cups of strained liquid into a large kettle. Add orange granules and next 3 ingredients. Mix well. Bring to a boil, stirring constantly. Boil 1 minute.

3. Stir in sugar to dissolve. Add butter. Bring to a boil, stirring constantly. Boil 1 minute. Remove from heat. Mix in mint extract.

4. Ladle into 4- or 8-ounce sterilized jars, filling to ⅛-inch from top. Wipe rims and seal. Process in a boiling-water bath for 5 minutes. Remove from water, cover jars with a towel, and let stand overnight.

Yield: about 4 cups jelly

3	cups chopped fresh orange mint, spearmint, or peppermint
3½	cups orange juice
¼	cup orange granules
2	tablespoons rice wine vinegar
1	(1¾-ounce) package fruit pectin
3	drops yellow food coloring
4	cups sugar
1	tablespoon butter or margarine
1	teaspoon mint extract

Mint steeped in water and refrigerated makes a refreshing summer drink by itself or it can be added to iced tea.

Summer

Rosemary Jelly

1   quart sweetened
    cranberry juice
10 (8- to 10-inch)
    sprigs fresh
    rosemary
1   (3- to 4-inch)
    cinnamon stick,
    broken into small
    pieces
8   whole cloves
1   (1¾-ounce)
    package fruit
    pectin
2   drops red food
    coloring
    (optional)
4   cups sugar
1   tablespoon butter
    or margarine
Sprigs of fresh
    rosemary for jars

1. Combine cranberry juice and rosemary in a saucepan. Bring to a boil. Cover and simmer 15 minutes. Cool. Strain juice.

2. Measure 3 cups of strained liquid into a large kettle. Add cinnamon and next 3 ingredients. Stir well to dissolve pectin. Bring to a boil, stirring constantly. Boil 1 minute.

3. Stir in sugar to dissolve. Add butter and bring to a boil, stirring constantly. Boil 1 minute. Remove from heat.

4. Ladle into 4- or 8-ounce sterilized jars, filling to ⅛-inch from top. Add 2 to 3 sprigs of fresh rosemary to each jar. Wipe rims and seal. Process in a boiling-water bath for 5 minutes. Remove from water, cover jars with a towel, and let stand overnight.

Yield: about 4 or 5 cups

Spread this jelly on your toasted bagel or serve alongside roast beef, pork, or lamb.

Fourth Of July Tea

Add leaves and blossoms of bee balm to your tea. The colonists learned to use bee balm or bergamot from the Indians who called it Oswego tea. Package dried applemint, bee balm, thyme, and rosemary. Tie with red, white, and blue ribbon. Use as favors at your Fourth of July Picnic.

Tarragon Marinade for Steak

1. Line a shallow baking dish with half of onion slices. Cut lemon in half and squeeze juice over onion. Put lemon rinds in dish.

2. Add garlic and next 4 ingredients. Combine vinegar, wine, and oil. Pour into dish.

3. Lay a steak in the marinade and top with remaining onion slices. Marinate 3 hours, basting frequently.

Yield: *about 2 cups marinade*

2 large onions, sliced, divided
1 lemon
5 cloves garlic
1 dried bay leaf
½ teaspoon dry mustard
1 teaspoon salt
Freshly ground black pepper to taste
3 tablespoons tarragon vinegar
½ cup red wine
1 cup olive oil

Nita's Special Steak Rub

1. Combine all ingredients. Store in a covered container until ready to use.

2. Rub over steaks before grilling or broiling.

Yield: ¼ cup (enough to season 4 or 5 steaks)

For extra flavor, place dill and other herbs of choice directly on coals while grilling.

1 tablespoon dried marjoram
1 tablespoon dried basil
2 teaspoons garlic powder
2 teaspoons dried thyme
1 teaspoon crushed dried rosemary
¾ teaspoon dried oregano

Summer

Herb Mixture for Beef Dishes

3 tablespoons dried
   sweet marjoram
3 tablespoons dried
   sweet basil
4 tablespoons dried
   parsley
2½ tablespoons dried
   chervil
3 tablespoons dried
   summer savory

 1. Crush herbs together. Store in a well-sealed container.

2. Use 1 teaspoon or more as a seasoning.

Yield: about 1 cup

Keep this mixture and the one for pork on hand to sprinkle on roasts, chops, steaks, and stir into casseroles, soups, and stews.

Herb Mixture for Pork Dishes

3 tablespoons dried
   sweet basil
2½ tablespoons dried
   sage
3 tablespoons dried
   rosemary
3 tablespoons dried
   summer savory

 Crush herbs together. Store in a well-sealed container.

2. Use 1 teaspoon or more as a seasoning.

Yield: about ¾ cup

 Scent the grill with sprigs of rosemary over hot coals just before food is done.

Black Bean Salsa

1. Partially drain beans. Mash about half of the beans.

2. Combine mashed and whole beans with salt and pepper, and remaining 4 ingredients. Chill for a few hours or overnight.

3. Serve with corn chips.

Yield: about 3½ cups

1   (15-ounce) can black beans
Salt and pepper to taste
¼   cup lime juice
¼   cup chopped fresh cilantro
2-3   tomatoes, chopped
5-6   green onions, chopped

David's Special Salsa

1. Combine vinegar and next 7 ingredients. Set aside.

2. Combine tomato and onion in a food processor. Using the "pulse" setting, blend until mixed but chunky. Do not puree.

3. Add spice mixture and blend to mix.

4. Refrigerate in a sealed container at least 24 hours before serving. Store in refrigerator or freezer. Serve with tortilla chips, preferably the unsalted or lightly salted varieties.

Yield: about 2 cups

2   tablespoons red wine vinegar
2   tablespoons hot water
1   teaspoon crushed red pepper flakes
¼   teaspoon chili powder
1   tablespoon fresh parley
1½   teaspoons dried cilantro
½   teaspoon dried thyme
¼   teaspoon garlic powder
3-4   medium tomatoes, chopped
½   medium onion, diced

Summer

Bean Salsa

1 (16-ounce) can corn, drained
1 (16-ounce) can garbanzo beans, drained
1 (15-ounce) can black beans, drained
1 (16-ounce) can dark red kidney beans, drained
1 cup chopped tomato
⅓ cup sliced green onion
2 tablespoons olive oil
3 tablespoons red wine vinegar
1 tablespoon fresh parsley
1½ teaspoons cumin
2 teaspoons dried oregano
1 teaspoon salt
½ teaspoon black pepper

1. Combine all ingredients and mix well.

2. Refrigerate several hours before serving.

Yield: about 10 cups

Painted Plant Pots

Sponge paint or stencil with permanent paints onto terra cotta pots. Paint matching garden tools and gloves to give as gifts.

Miss Karen's Great Salsa

 1. Combine all ingredients in a blender. Puree.

2. Serve with tortilla chips.

Yield: about 3 to 3½ cups

This salsa makes a good topping for baked potatoes or poached fish.

5   medium tomatoes, peeled
½   cup fresh cilantro
4   green onions, chopped
¼   teaspoon chili powder
½   teaspoon sliced jalapeño pepper
Garlic salt to taste

Basil Pesto

 1. Combine all ingredients in a food processor or blender. Turning the machine on and off rapidly, pulse the mixture several times until coarsely chopped. Scrape down sides. Continue to pulse until mixture is smooth.

Yield: about 3½ to 4 cups

This sauce is excellent as a topping for fresh tomatoes, cheese slices, or hot pasta. Use it also as a seasoning for tomato sauces, as a dip, or as a meat baste.

¾   cup walnuts
3   cups stemmed and packed fresh basil leaves
1½ cups olive oil
1   cup Parmesan cheese
4   medium cloves garlic

 Traditionally, basil was considered both a symbol of hate and misfortune, as well as used as a love charm.

Summer

Arugula Pesto

6 cups fresh arugula leaves, washed and dried
2 cloves garlic
1½ cups walnuts
½ teaspoon salt
¾ cup Parmesan cheese
⅓ cup olive oil

1. Blend arugula leaves and garlic in a food processor. Add walnuts, salt, and cheese. Continue to process while slowly adding oil. Mix well.

2. Freeze if not used within 1 week.

Yield: about 2 cups

Toss pesto with hot cooked pasta or mix with cream cheese to make a spread for crackers.

Dill Pesto

1 cup fresh dill
½ cup fresh parsley
¼ cup Parmesan cheese
¼ cup almonds or walnuts
2 cloves garlic
½ cup oil
½ teaspoon salt
1 cup grated Swiss cheese

1. Combine dill and next 6 ingredients in a food processor or blender. Process until coarsely pureed.

2. Add cheese and process until mixed. Add extra oil if consistency is too thick.

Yield: about 1½ cups

Substitute 2 tablespoons dried dill and increase parsley to 1 cup if fresh dill is not available.

Sage Pesto

1. Combine sage and next 7 ingredients in a food processor. Process until nuts are finely chopped but not pureed.

2. Transfer mixture to a bowl. Fold in 2 cups cheese.

3. Use 1 cup pesto for each pound of dry pasta prepared. Garnish.

Yield: 3 to 4 cups

Unused pesto stores well in a freezer for several months.

¾ cup coarsely chopped fresh sage leaves
1 cup vegetable oil
¾ cup walnut oil
½ cup peanut oil
1½ cups hazelnuts, toasted
1 cup walnuts, toasted
1½ tablespoons chopped garlic
1 teaspoon ground allspice
2 cups freshly grated Parmesan cheese
Parmesan cheese for garnish

Sorrel Pesto

1. Blend sorrel and next 6 ingredients in a food processor or blender. Continue to process while slowly adding oil.

2. Refrigerate or freeze. Serve with pasta or as a dip.

Yield: about 1½ cups

1½ cups stemmed fresh sorrel leaves
½ cup fresh parsley
1 tablespoon fresh oregano, or 1 teaspoon dried
Zest of 2 lemons
¼ cup almonds
½ cup Parmesan cheese
½ teaspoon salt
¾ cup olive oil

Summer

Lime and Cilantro Vinaigrette

3 tablespoons lime
   juice
2 tablespoons white
   wine vinegar
2 tablespoons fresh
   cilantro
1 tablespoon ground
   ginger
1 clove garlic,
   chopped
⅓ cup vegetable oil
1 tablespoon olive
   oil
Salt and pepper

 1. Whip lime juice and next 4 ingredients together in a small bowl.

2. Slowly beat in vegetable oil, then olive oil. Season with salt and pepper.

Yield: 1 serving

Forget the same old salad dressings. This flavor combination goes with the season's greens or with a vegetable tray as a dipping sauce.

Iced Mint Tea

9 cups water,
   divided
12 large sprigs fresh
   mint, plus extra
   for garnish
4 (¼-ounce) tea
   bags
1 cup orange juice
¼ cup lemon juice
1 cup sugar
Orange slices for
   garnish

1. Bring 3 cups water to a boil. Remove from heat and add mint and tea bags. Cool and strain.

2. Combine orange juice, lemon juice, sugar, and remaining 6 cups water. Stir to dissolve sugar. Add to tea.

3. Pour over ice and garnish.

Yield: 6 to 8 servings

Refreshing Mint Tea

1. Place tea bags in a 1-gallon container. Boil water. Pour water over tea bags. Add sugar and mint and let steep for 30 minutes.

2. Remove tea bags and add lemonade and limeade. Add enough water to make 1 gallon of tea. Chill.

3. Serve over ice with garnish.

Yield: 20 servings

2	(¼-ounce) tea bags
3	cups water
1½	cups sugar
8-10	sprigs fresh mint, plus extra for garnish
1	(6-ounce) can frozen lemonade concentrate
1	(6-ounce) can frozen limeade concentrate
	Lemon slices for garnish

Orange Mint Punch

1. Combine mint, honey, and 2 cups water in a large saucepan. Simmer 10 minutes over low heat. Remove from heat.

2. Bring remaining 12 cups water to a boil in a separate saucepan. Add tea bags and boiling water to mint mixture. Allow to steep for about 30 minutes. Remove tea bags and add orange juice. Refrigerate until cold.

3. To serve, pour tea over an ice cube with a sprig of fresh mint frozen inside.

Yield: 6 to 8 servings

1	cup fresh orange mint leaves
2	tablespoons honey
14	cups water, divided
6	decaffeinated tea bags
1	(12-ounce) can frozen orange juice concentrate

Summer

Yvonne's Wedding Bell Punch

6 cups water
1½ cups sugar
1 (3-ounce) package strawberry-flavored jello
½ cup lemon juice
2½ cups orange juice
1 (16-ounce) package frozen strawberries, thawed and pureed
4 cups unsweetened pineapple juice
1 (2-liter) bottle ginger ale
Fresh lavender and sprigs of fresh rosemary for garnish

1. Bring water to a boil. Add sugar and jello and stir to dissolve. Mix in lemon juice, orange juice, and strawberries. Freeze.

2. Add pineapple juice and ginger ale when ready to serve. Garnish.

Yield: 20 servings

Summer Cooler

2 cups water
2 cups sugar
Juice of 6 lemons
Juice of 2 oranges
½ cup chopped fresh mint
1 quart ginger ale

1. Boil water and sugar 5 minutes. Pour over juices and mint.

2. Place 3 tablespoons of mixture in a glass. Fill with crushed ice. Add ginger ale. Store remaining syrup in refrigerator.

Yield: 6 to 8 servings

Elderberry Syrup

1. Combine blossoms and next 4 ingredients in a plastic container. Let stand for 24 hours.

2. Put mixture through a sieve to remove blossoms and fruit. Add sugar to strained mixture, stirring until sugar dissolves.

3. Pour into bottles and store in a cool place; refrigerate if possible. Use within 2 to 3 months for peak flavor.

Yield: *about 5 quarts*

Mix with sparkling water for a refreshing and unusual drink. Place sprigs of fresh lemon balm or lemon verbena in glass when served.

In eastern Austria, the syrup is mixed with sparkling water and considered a drink to good health.

60	large elderberry blossoms
6	lemons, sliced
6	oranges, sliced
4	ounces citric acid
5	quarts water
2½	pounds sugar

Aloe Gift Basket

Make a basket of aloe plant, soap, and lotion and enclose a card telling something about your herb gift. Legend tells us aloe was Cleopatra's beauty secret. Your plant will grow on the kitchen windowsill. Water sparingly in the winter. For small burns or cuts simply cut a piece from one of the leaves and apply the sap directly to the affected area.

Summer

Soups & Salads

Green Vichyssoise

2 cups sliced leeks
4 tablespoons butter
4 medium potatoes, peeled and diced
4 cups chicken broth
½ cup chopped fresh parsley, celery tops, spinach, or tarragon
1 cup cream or milk
Salt and pepper to taste

1. Sauté leeks in butter in a 3-quart saucepan. Add potatoes. Pour in broth and cook until potatoes are tender.

2. Place fresh herbs in a blender. Pour broth mixture over top. Blend until coarsely pureed. Stir in cream. Add salt and pepper. Chill before serving.

Yield: *about 6 servings*

For a luncheon, use old herb bottles as holders filled with several kinds of herbs (and tiny flowers) from your garden. They will be delightful gifts for your guests to take home.

Garden Gazpacho

1. Reserve 5 pieces of celery, 2 pieces of bell pepper, 1 piece of cucumber, and 4 pieces of tomato.

2. Combine remaining celery, pepper, and cucumber with onion in a food processor. Process until finely chopped.

3. Remove to a non-metallic bowl. Process tomatoes until smooth. Add parsley and garlic and continue to process until smooth. Add mixture to bowl.

4. Mix in vinegar and next 5 ingredients. Process reserved vegetables on the "pulse" setting 2 to 3 times or until coarsely chopped. Gently fold into bowl mixture. Refrigerate overnight.

5. Garnish and serve very cold.

Yield: 6 to 8 servings

Tomato juice may replace some of tomatoes.

6 stalks celery, cut into 1-inch pieces, divided
2 bell peppers, cut into eighths, divided
1 large cucumber, cut into sixths, divided
2 quarts peeled and quartered tomatoes, divided
1 medium onion, cut into eighths
2 tablespoons chopped fresh parsley
2 cloves garlic
½ cup white wine vinegar
2½ teaspoons salt, or to taste
1 teaspoon black pepper
1½ teaspoons Worcestershire sauce
½ teaspoon hot pepper sauce
2 tablespoons fresh basil leaves
Chopped fresh chives for garnish.

Summer

Tomato Basil Soup

2 large onions, minced
6 stalks celery, minced
4 tablespoons butter
6 ounces tomato puree
1 tablespoon sugar
2 quarts vegetable juice
1 tablespoon Worcestershire sauce
1 teaspoon hot pepper sauce
1 teaspoon salt
1 teaspoon celery salt
¼ teaspoon black pepper
2 tablespoons lemon juice
1 tablespoon dried basil
¼ cup Parmesan cheese
Beef consommé

1. Sauté onion and celery in butter in a large saucepan.

2. Add tomato puree and next 10 ingredients. Simmer 60 minutes.

3. Thin with beef consommé, if desired.

Yield: 4 to 6 servings

A dog scarf made of a bandana folded into a triangle then stuffed with dried pennyroyal keeps fleas off your pet.

Spicy Tomato Soup

1. In a covered saucepan, steam onion, garlic, and water until tender. Remove from heat and stir in flour.

2. Add milk slowly and stir to blend. Add tomato and next 6 ingredients. Simmer uncovered 20 minutes, stirring occasionally.
3. Serve as is or pureed. Serve hot or cold. Top each serving with a dollop of sour cream and garnish. Serve with garlic cheese toast.

Yield: 2 servings

1 onion, chopped
1 clove garlic, minced
2 tablespoons water
¼ cup all-purpose flour
½ cup low-fat milk
4 tomatoes, peeled, seeded, and chopped
2 teaspoons chicken bouillon
¼ cup chopped fresh basil
1 teaspoon sugar
½ teaspoon salt
¼ teaspoon dried dill
¼ teaspoon black pepper
Sour cream or yogurt
Dried dill for garnish

Happy Kitchen Wreath

Take long stems of herbs and form into a circle. Tie a bow of raffia at top with a garlic bulb and two dried red peppers hanging in the center. Makes the kitchen smell good and you can use the "parts" as needed.

Summer

Zucchini Soup

1 large yellow onion, thinly sliced
1 teaspoon olive oil
4 medium to large zucchini, cut in chunks
2 carrots, cut in small chunks
2 stalks celery with leaves, chopped
1 teaspoon salt
½ teaspoon black pepper
1 tablespoon Italian seasoning
3 large cloves garlic, chopped
1 quart water
1 cup dry white wine (optional)
Sprigs of fresh parsley for garnish

1. In a large pot, sauté onion in oil until soft. Add zucchini and next 7 ingredients. Cover and simmer 30 minutes.

2. Let cool until warm. Place in a blender and puree. Stir in wine. Adjust seasoning as needed. Serve warm or at room temperature. Garnish.

Yield: 4 servings

Mandarin Orange Salad With Lemon Balm

1. Combine mayonnaise and next 4 ingredients. Stir well and set aside.

2. To prepare salad, measure reserved pineapple and orange juice. Add enough water to make 1½ cups. Dissolve gelatin in tea. Add juice.

3. Chill until mixture thickens to the consistency of unbeaten egg whites. Fold in pineapple, oranges, and water chestnuts. Pour into a lightly greased 13x9x2-inch pan. Chill until firm.

4. Serve over lemon balm leaves or with leaves on the side. Spoon dressing over individual servings.

Yield: 10 to 12 servings

Serve this refreshing salad during a hot summer's night meal.

Dressing

- ½ cup mayonnaise
- ¼ cup heavy cream
- 1 tablespoon orange zest
- 1 teaspoon sugar
- ¼ teaspoon ground mace

Salad

- 1 (15¼-ounce) can crushed pineapple, juice reserved
- 1 (11-ounce) can mandarin oranges, juice reserved
- 1 (6-ounce) package orange-flavored gelatin
- 1½ cups hot tea
- 1 (8-ounce) can sliced water chestnuts, drained
- Fresh lemon balm leaves for garnish
- Dressing (optional)

Summer

Hayden Salad

1 gallon ripe tomatoes
1 gallon cabbage
1 quart onions
6 bell peppers
1 cup salt
3 tablespoons dry mustard
2 tablespoons ground ginger
1 teaspoon ground cloves
1 teaspoon celery seed
1 teaspoon cinnamon
3 pounds sugar
2 quarts vinegar

1. Grind together tomatoes and next 3 ingredients. Add salt and let stand 2 hours.

2. Drain vegetables. Mix in mustard and remaining 6 ingredients. Cook about 30 minutes.

3. Pack into sterilized jars and seal. Process in a boiling-water bath for 20 minutes.

Yield: about 20 pints

This was a famous and well-circulated relish recipe over 100 years ago in the Memphis Conference of the Methodist Church.

 Use nasturtium leaves and stems and dill and fennel fronds as tender greens for salads.

Arugula, Lettuce, and Orange Salad With Walnuts

1. Combine arugula and lettuce in salad bowl. Refrigerate.

2. Peel oranges and divide into sections. Remove membrane from each section. Recover juice that results during this process. Put sections and juice in a bowl, cover, and refrigerate.

3. Combine lemon juice and next 5 ingredients. Blend well. Taste for proper seasoning. Dressing should be slightly sweet. Add some of dressing to greens. Toss. Add more dressing, as needed.

4. Arrange orange sections on lettuce. Sprinkle walnut pieces over top. Dust with extra cinnamon. Serve immediately.

Yield: 6 to 8 servings

Leftover dressing stores well in the refrigerator for a few days.

4 cups chopped arugula
6 cups chopped Iceberg or Romaine lettuce
4 navel oranges, or 1 (11-ounce) can mandarin oranges, drained
¼ cup lemon juice
2 tablespoons sugar
½ cup orange juice
Pinch of salt
½ teaspoon cinnamon
1 tablespoons orange flower water (optional)
1 cup walnut pieces, toasted

Antique handkerchiefs make lovely potpourri bags.

Summer

Black-eyed Pea Salad

1 (16-ounce) package dried black-eyed peas
6 cups water
1 (6-ounce) jar marinated artichoke hearts
2 cups cooked rotelle macaroni
1 medium-size green bell pepper, chopped
1 medium-size red bell pepper, chopped
¾ cup canned garbanzo beans
½ cup chopped red onion
6 ounces sliced provolone cheese, cut into strips
3½ ounces sliced pepperoni, cut into strips
3 tablespoon chopped fresh parsley
1 (0.7-ounce) package Italian salad dressing mix
¼ cup sugar
½ teaspoon black pepper
½ cup vinegar
¼ cup vegetable oil

1. Wash and sort peas. Place peas in a large Dutch oven and add enough water to cover 2 inches above top of peas. Soak 8 hours.

2. Drain peas. Add 6 cups water and bring to a boil. Reduce heat and cover. Simmer 45 minutes or until tender.

3. Drain peas and cool. Drain artichokes, reserving liquid. Chop artichokes.

4. Combine peas, artichoke, macaroni, and next 7 ingredients in a large bowl. Toss gently.

5. Place reserved artichoke liquid, dressing mix, and remaining 4 ingredients in a jar. Cover tightly and shake vigorously. Pour over pea mixture. Mix gently. Cover and chill at least 2 hours.

Yield: 12 servings

Broccoli Salad

1. Cook broccoli in boiling water for about 3 minutes. Plunge into cold water and drain.

2. Combine broccoli with onion and mushrooms. Mix together mayonnaise, lemon juice, and anchovy paste. Toss with vegetable mixture. Add black pepper and dill.

3. If made in advance, let broccoli marinate in mayonnaise mixture in refrigerator, but wait until just before serving to add onion and mushrooms.

Yield: 6 to 8 servings

This dish is great for summer picnics. Add fresh spinach and sliced water chestnuts for variety.

2 bunches broccoli, cut into flowerettes
1 small red onion, thinly sliced
1 pound mushrooms, sliced
1 cup mayonnaise
Juice of ½ lemon
½ teaspoon anchovy paste, or to taste
Freshly ground black pepper to taste
2 teaspoons dried dill, or 1 tablespoon minced fresh

Cold Cauliflower Salad

1. Cut cauliflower and radishes into bite-size pieces.

2. Combine with water chestnuts and remaining 5 ingredients.

3. Refrigerate overnight.

Yield: 4 to 6 servings

1 whole cauliflower
1 cup radishes
1 (8-ounce) can sliced water chestnuts
½ cup chopped onion
¾ cup mayonnaise
¾ cup sour cream
1 (0.4-ounce) package dry ranch dressing mix
Fresh dill to taste

Summer

Cool-as-a-Cucumber Salad

1   medium to large
tomato, cored
⅓   medium onion
½   large cucumber,
thinly sliced
5   fresh basil leaves,
sliced
2   tablespoons sugar
½   cup vinegar of
choice
Salt to taste

1. Cut tomato into large chunks. Chop or slice onion into large pieces.

2. Combine tomato, onion, cucumber, and basil in a bowl. Add sugar. Mix in vinegar. Cover with cold water. Add salt to enhance the flavor.

Yield: 3 to 4 servings

Parsley Salad

1   heaping cup fresh
parsley, chopped
4-5   small sun-dried
tomatoes in oil,
drained
4-5   shavings fresh
Parmesan cheese
Balsamic vinaigrette

1. Toss all ingredients together.

Yield: 1 serving

This salad is an amazingly good combination of flavors. It is wonderful in the summer with fresh garden ingredients, but is also good in winter with today's readily available fresh produce at supermarkets.

Glue dried herbs and flowers on a
ribbon and tie around a straw hat.

Cornbread Salad

1. Combine dressing mix, sour cream, and mayonnaise; set aside.

2. Combine tomato and next 4 ingredients; set aside.

3. Assemble salad by crumbling half of cornbread in the bottom of a large bowl. In layers, spread half of beans and half of next 4 ingredients over cornbread. Top with half of tomato mixture and half of dressing mixture. Crumble remaining cornbread into bowl. Repeat layers, reserving a small amount of Cheddar cheese and tomato mixture to sprinkle over top of final dressing layer.

Yield: 8 to 10 servings

This is an attractive salad and great for serving a crowd.When preparing the cornbread for the recipe, try adding green chiles to the batter.

1 (1-ounce) package dry ranch dressing mix
1 cup sour cream
1 cup mayonnaise
5 large tomatoes, seeded and chopped
1 tablespoon chopped jalapeño pepper
½ bell pepper, chopped
2 green onions, chopped
½ cup chopped fresh cilantro
1 pan cornbread
2 (16-ounce) cans pinto beans, drained
5 ounces Cheddar cheese, grated
1 (3-ounce) jar real bacon bits
2 (15¼-ounce) cans corn, drained
5 ounces Monterey Jack cheese, grated

Summer

Red and White Bean Salad With Avocado, Bacon, and Basil

Dressing

1   cup vegetable or olive oil
¼   cup lemon juice or white wine vinegar
¼   cup water
⅓   cup fresh parsley
2   tablespoons fresh marjoram or mild fresh oregano
1   tablespoon fresh thyme
1   teaspoon freshly ground coriander
1   teaspoon cumin seed
1   large clove garlic, cut in several pieces
1   teaspoon salt
⅛   teaspoon hot pepper sauce
1   tablespoon Dijon or grainy-type mustard

1. Combine oil and next 11 ingredients in a food processor or blender. Process until smooth. Taste for proper seasoning. Add extra salt and lemon juice as needed.

Red and White Bean Salad With Avocado, Bacon, and Basil (continued)

2. To prepare salad, dice bacon and cook until crisp. Drain. Drain beans, rinse, and drain well. Combine beans, salt, pepper, and next 4 ingredients. Moisten with dressing. Chill.

3. Just before serving, sprinkle with bacon. Garnish.

Yield: 1½ cups dressing

Dip avocado in lemon juice to prevent browning if preparing ahead. Slice or tear basil just before combining in salad with dressing.

Variation: Substitute freshly cooked dried beans for canned. Cook red and white beans separately. To prepare, soak beans according to package. Drain. Add chicken broth or water to cover beans. Mix in 2 cloves garlic, 1 medium onion, chopped, and 2 to 3 table-spoons olive oil. Bring to a boil. Reduce heat and cover. Cook until tender, adding extra liquid as needed to keep beans covered. Add salt and pepper when almost done cooking.

Madalene Hill and Gwen Barclay
Copyright © 1992

Salad

4-6	slices bacon
1	(15¼-ounce) can red kidney beans
1	(15-ounce) can white kidney beans (cannellini beans)
	Salt and freshly ground black pepper to taste
1	bunch green onions, sliced
1	large avocado, peeled and diced
½	cup whole Greek black olives, or ¼ cup sliced
½	cup sliced or torn fresh basil
½-⅔	cup dressing
	Sprigs of fresh basil for garnish

Summer

Ensalada Verde

Salad

2	avocados, peeled and sliced
1	large cucumber, thinly sliced
1	cup pimiento-stuffed Spanish olives
1	(14½-ounce) can cut green beans, drained
1	(15-ounce) can green peas, drained
1	(15-ounce) can asparagus spears, drained
½	cup olive oil
2	tablespoons herbal vinegar
1	clove garlic, halved
1	teaspoon dry mustard
1	teaspoon salt
1	teaspoon dill
¼	teaspoon black pepper

Garlic Sauce

2	egg yolks
6	cloves garlic, crushed
1	cup olive oil
	Juice of 1 lemon
	Salt and pepper to taste

1. Arrange avocados and next 5 ingredients on a serving platter or combine in a bowl.

2. Combine olive oil and next 6 ingredients. Blend well. Pour over vegetables. Chill several hours.

3. Prepare garlic sauce just before serving by beating egg yolks and garlic together. Using a fork or whip, slowly beat in oil and lemon juice. Season as needed with salt and pepper. Pour over salad.

Yield: 6 to 8 servings

Basil Potato Salad

1. Boil potatoes until tender. Cool and cut into quarters.

2. Combine mayonnaise and remaining 7 ingredients. Pour over potatoes. Chill.

Yield: 8 servings

The season's favorite salad is mixed with a creamy dressing that may become your season's standard.

2 pounds red potatoes, unpeeled
⅔ cup light mayonnaise
½ cup low-fat sour cream
¼ cup milk
2 tablespoons Dijon mustard
1 teaspoon salt
¾ teaspoon freshly ground black pepper
¼ cup chopped fresh parsley
1 cup shredded fresh basil leaves

Dill Potato Salad

1. Boil potatoes until tender. Cool, peel, and cut into cubes.

2. Sprinkle onion and next 3 ingredients over potato.

3. Add mayonnaise and gently stir. Refrigerate several hours or overnight.

Yield: 6 to 8 servings

6 medium potatoes
2 tablespoons finely chopped onion
1 tablespoon chopped fresh chives
1 tablespoon chopped fresh parsley
3 tablespoons chopped fresh dill
6 tablespoons mayonnaise

Summer

Herbal Potato Salad

6   medium to large potatoes, unpeeled
1   teaspoon salt
2   hard-cooked eggs, chopped
1   medium pickle, chopped
½   medium onion, chopped
1   small carrot, chopped
1   stalk celery with leaves, chopped
⅓   cup chopped fresh garlic or onion chives
5   tablespoons chopped fresh rosemary
3   tablespoons chopped fresh thyme
⅓   cup chopped fresh parsley
⅓   cup light mayonnaise
2   teaspoons Worcestershire sauce
Salt to taste
6   lettuce leaves

1. Cut potatoes into large chunks. Boil with 1 teaspoon salt for 10 minutes or until tender. Drain and cover with cold water to cool slightly.

2. Drain potatoes. Chop into smaller chunks. Add egg and next 8 ingredients.

3. Combine mayonnaise and Worcestershire sauce. Add to potato mixture. Stir together. Add salt.

4. Serve salad on lettuce leaves.

Yield: 6 servings

Substitute cole slaw dressing for mayonnaise and Worcestershire sauce for a slightly sweeter variation.

Mediterranean Potato Salad

1. Process oil and next 8 ingredients in a blender to make a dressing; set aside.

2. Cover potatoes with water in a saucepan and bring to a boil. Reduce heat and simmer 10 minutes or until tender. Drain.

3. Place warm potatoes in a salad bowl. Pour dressing over them. Cool.

4. Add garbanzo beans and remaining 4 ingredients. Toss. Serve at room temperature.

Yield: 6 to 8 servings

⅔ cup oil
⅓ cup red wine vinegar
½ teaspoon anchovy paste
1 teaspoon dried oregano
1 tablespoon dried parsley
1 tablespoon mayonnaise
1 large clove garlic
1 teaspoon salt
½ teaspoon black pepper
1½ pounds new potatoes, quartered
1 (16-ounce) can garbanzo beans
8 ounces feta cheese, crumbled
¼ cup pitted kalamata olives
½ cup diced red onion
1 cup diced tomato

Louise's Skinny Potato Salad

1. Cook potatoes until tender. Drain.

2. Pour dressing over warm potatoes. Add herbs. Mix well and chill.

Yield: 8 to 10 servings

2 pounds red potatoes, cubed
1 (8-ounce) bottle low-fat Italian dressing
1 cup fresh herbs of choice

Summer

Tabbouleh

1 cup bulgar
1 large head romaine lettuce
¼ cup olive oil
¼ cup lemon juice
2 teaspoons salt
1½ teaspoons ground allspice
2 medium tomatoes, diced
1 cup finely chopped green onions, including tops
1 cup finely chopped fresh parsley
½ cup finely chopped fresh mint

1. Cook or soak bulgar according to package. Drain and set aside.

2. Clean lettuce and separate leaves. Chill.

3. Combine oil and next 3 ingredients to make a dressing.

4. Mix together bulgar, dressing, tomato, and next 3 ingredients.

5. Line a platter with the largest lettuce leaves. Place bulgar mixture in center. Put remaining lettuce leaves on a separate platter.

6. To eat, tear off a piece of lettuce and use it to scoop up the tabbouleh. Wrap piece of lettuce around the tabbouleh and enjoy.

Yield: 6 to 8 servings

Prepare ahead and refrigerate, if desired. Assemble platters just before serving.

Summer Bulgar Salad

¾ cup bulgar
1½ cups chicken broth
½ cup chopped fresh parsley
1 medium tomato, seeded and chopped
¼ cup lemon juice
¼ cup olive oil
1 tablespoon chopped mint
¼ teaspoon black pepper
Fresh tomatoes, sliced

1. Cook bulgar in broth until tender. Drain.

2. Combine bulgar with parsley and next 5 ingredients. Cover and refrigerate at least 4 hours, preferably overnight.

3. Serve over sliced tomatoes.

Yield: 4 to 6 servings

Side Dishes

Cherry Tomatoes Provençal

 1. Place tomatoes in a single layer in a lightly greased shallow pan.

2. Combine onion and remaining 7 ingredients. Sprinkle over tomatoes.

3. Bake at 425° for 6 to 8 minutes or until tomatoes are tender and breadcrumbs begin to brown.

Yield: 4 servings

1	pint cherry tomatoes
¼	cup finely minced onion
1	clove garlic, finely minced
¼	cup chopped fresh parsley
¼	teaspoon crumbled dried thyme, or 1 tablespoon fresh
½	cup soft breadcrumbs
½	teaspoon salt
	Black pepper to taste
¼	cup olive oil

Time-honored herb combinations: basil for tomatoes; marjoram or tarragon for poultry; rosemary for lamb or beef.

Summer

Tomato Basil Compote

1½ tablespoons olive oil
2 cloves garlic, peeled and thinly sliced
1½ pints cherry tomatoes, any color
Salt and pepper, to taste
8 large fresh basil leaves

1. Heat oil in a large skillet over medium-low heat. Add garlic and sauté 3 minutes or until soft and golden.

2. Add tomatoes, salt, and pepper. Cook, stirring often, 3 to 5 minutes or until tomatoes are just warm and ready to burst.

3. Add basil and cook 1 minute.

Yield: 4 servings

The natural pairing of tomato and basil is a welcome addition to grilled pork or lamb.

Tarragon Tomatoes

5 tomatoes
Sugar
¾ cup grated cheese of choice
½ cup breadcrumbs
½ teaspoon salt
⅛ teaspoon freshly ground black pepper
½ teaspoon dried tarragon, or 1 teaspoon fresh

1. Cut tomatoes in half. Arrange, cut side up, in a shallow baking dish that is an appropriate size to snugly fit halves. Sprinkle halves lightly with sugar. Top halves with cheese.

2. Combine breadcrumbs and remaining 3 ingredients. Sprinkle mixture over cheese.

3. Bake uncovered at 375° for about 30 minutes.

Yield: 6 to 8 servings

Aunt Lizzy's Eggplant

1. Brown beef over medium heat in a large skillet. Add onion and garlic. Cook and stir to break up meat. Drain fat.

2. Mix in coriander and next 7 ingredients. Cook 3 to 4 minutes.

3. Add tomato and ½ cup of reserved juice. Reduce heat and simmer 30 minutes.

4. Cut eggplant into 1-inch cubes. Heat oil over medium-high heat in a second skillet. Sauté eggplant in small batches until lightly browned. Remove with a slotted spoon and drain on paper towels. Add eggplant to meat mixture. Simmer 20 to 30 minutes or until eggplant is tender. Add extra tomato juice if mixture becomes too dry. Remove bay leaf. Adjust seasonings as desired.

5. Serve with steamed rice and unleavened bread.

Yield: 4 to 6 servings

1 pound lean ground beef
1 medium onion, chopped
1 clove garlic, minced
2 teaspoons ground coriander
1 dried bay leaf
½ teaspoon turmeric
½ teaspoon ground cumin
½ teaspoon cinnamon
2 whole cloves
Pinch of salt
Cayenne pepper to taste
1 (16-ounce) can tomatoes, drained and chopped, juice reserved
1 medium eggplant
¼ cup olive oil
Steamed rice and unleavened bread

Cajun Eggplant

2 large eggplants
1 medium onion, chopped
1 stalk celery, chopped, or 1 small bunch lovage
1 cup diced fresh tomatoes, or 1 (16-ounce) can
½ teaspoon fresh thyme
½ teaspoon cayenne pepper, or to taste
1 tablespoon dried parsley
Cooked shrimp or crabmeat to taste (optional)
4 ounces Cheddar cheese, grated, divided

1. Slice eggplants in half lengthwise. Scoop out center. Boil centers until transparent. Drain.

2. Sauté onion and next 5 ingredients until onion and celery become transparent.

3. In eggplant shells, layer 2 ounces cheese, eggplant, sautéed vegetables, seafood, and remaining 2 ounces cheese.

4. Bake at 350° for 30 minutes or until cheese is bubbly.

Yield: 4 servings

Arrange several old herb bottles on the kitchen counter to fill with herbs and blossoms (Lilliput Zinnias are knockouts). The herbs are handy too if you're in a hurry and need a quick snip for a recipe.

Summer Squash Casserole

1. Boil squash and onion in salted water for 5 minutes. Drain.

2. Combine soup and sour cream. Stir in carrot. Fold in cooked vegetables.

3. In a separate bowl, combine stuffing mix and butter. Spread half of stuffing mixture in a 13x9x2-inch glass casserole dish. Spoon vegetable mixture over top. Sprinkle with remaining stuffing mixture.

4. Bake at 350° for 25 to 30 minutes or until heated thoroughly.

Yield: 8 servings

2 pounds crookneck squash, sliced
¼ cup chopped onion
1 (10¾-ounce) can condensed cream of chicken soup
1 cup sour cream
1 cup grated carrot
1 (8-ounce) package herb-seasoned stuffing mix
1 stick butter or margarine, melted

Basil Zucchini

1. Sauté zucchini and garlic in oil until tender.

2. Add tomato, basil, and marjoram. Cook and stir 3 to 5 minutes.

3. Top each serving with cheese.

Yield: 4 servings

To reduce fat, coat sauté pan with nonstick cooking spray and decrease oil to 1 teaspoon.

2 cups sliced zucchini
1 clove garlic, minced
2 tablespoons olive oil
1 cup chopped tomato
1 teaspoon chopped fresh basil leaves
½ teaspoon chopped fresh marjoram leaves
Parmesan cheese

Summer

Sweet-and-Sour Yellow Squash With Mint

1   pound yellow
    squash or zucchini
2   tablespoons
    vegetable oil
1   medium onion,
    chopped
Salt and freshly
    ground pepper
1½ tablespoons
    strained fresh
    lemon juice,
    divided
⅓   cup water
1   teaspoon dried
    chocolate mint,
    crumbled
2   large cloves garlic,
    minced
2   teaspoons sugar or
    honey
Sprig of fresh
    chocolate mint for
    garnish

1. Cut squash into ½-inch slices; set aside.

2. Heat oil in a medium skillet. Add onion and sauté over medium heat 5 minutes or until golden brown.

3. Add squash, salt, and pepper and sauté 2 minutes. Add 1 tablespoon lemon juice and next 4 ingredients. Cover and cook, stirring occasionally, over medium heat 7 minutes or until squash is tender. Add a small amount of water, if needed, during cooking.

4. Remove from heat and mix in remaining ½ tablespoon lemon juice. Add more seasonings, if desired. Serve hot or cold. Garnish.

Yield: 4 to 6 servings

This summer vegetable pleaser is yet another reason to give over a corner of the garden to versatile, surprising mint.

Summer

Dilled Scalloped Zucchini

1. Coat a shallow casserole dish with nonstick cooking spray. Spread zucchini in bottom of dish.

2. Combine mayonnaise, garlic, and dill. Cover zucchini with mayonnaise mixture.

3. Bake uncovered at 375° for 25 to 30 minutes. Mix breadcrumbs and cheese. Sprinkle over top and bake 15 minutes more.

Yield: 5 or 6 servings

- 4 cups sliced zucchini
- ½ cup light mayonnaise
- 2 cloves garlic, pressed
- 1 teaspoon dried dill, or 1 heaping tablespoon fresh
- ½ cup Italian-style breadcrumbs
- ¼ cup Parmesan cheese

Herb Butter Zucchini Fans

1. Combine butter and next 4 ingredients; set aside.

2. Cut lengthwise slices into each zucchini, leaving slices attached at stem end. Fan slices out and spread evenly with butter mixture.

3. Place in a 15x10x1-inch jellyroll pan. Add water.

4. Bake at 400° for 20 minutes or until crisp-tender.

5. Combine cheese and breadcrumbs. Sprinkle over zucchini. Broil 4 inches from heat for 2 minutes or until cheese melts.

Yield: 4 servings

- 5 tablespoons butter or margarine, softened
- 2 tablespoons minced fresh parsley
- ½ teaspoon dried tarragon
- ⅛ teaspoon salt
- ⅛ teaspoon black pepper
- 4 small zucchini
- ¼ cup water
- 2 tablespoons Parmesan cheese
- 1 tablespoon soft breadcrumbs

Summer

Basil Tomato Tart

1½ cups grated mozzarella cheese, divided
1 (9-inch) baked pie shell
5 Roma or 4 regular medium tomatoes
1 cup loosely packed fresh basil leaves
4 cloves garlic
½ cup mayonnaise
¼ cup Parmesan
⅛ teaspoon white pepper
Chopped fresh basil leaves for garnish

1. Sprinkle ½ cup mozzarella cheese on bottom of pie shell.

2. Cut tomatoes in wedges and drain on a paper towel. Arrange wedges on cheese.

3. Process basil and garlic in a food processor until coarsely chopped. Sprinkle over wedges.

4. Combine remaining 1 cup mozzarella cheese, mayonnaise, Parmesan cheese, and pepper. Spoon evenly over basil mixture to cover the top.

5. Bake at 375° for 35 to 40 minutes. Serve warm. Garnish.

Yield: 4 main dish servings or 8 appetizers

Zucchini Patties

3 cups grated zucchini
1 cup grated onion
1 large clove garlic, crushed
1 teaspoon salt
¼ teaspoon pepper
1 egg, lightly beaten
3 heaping tablespoons all-purpose flour
Pinch of dried thyme
1 tablespoon dried parsley
1 cup grated cheese

1. Combine all ingredients except cheese.

2. Drop large tablespoons of mixture into hot oil and fry until brown on all sides.

3. Sprinkle with cheese and cover until cheese melts.

Yield: 4 to 6 servings

If you're a gardener blessed with zucchini, just add ingenuity with herbs and supper is ready.

Zucchini Pie

1. Sauté zucchini, onion, and bell pepper in margarine for 10 minutes or until tender.

2. Stir in parsley and next 5 ingredients.

3. In a large bowl, combine egg and cheese. Stir in vegetables.

4. Spread mustard over bottom of pie shell. Pour mixture into shell.

5. Bake at 375° for 18 to 20 minutes or until a knife inserted near center comes out clean. Remove from oven and let stand 10 minutes before serving.

Yield: 6 to 8 servings

4   cups sliced unpeeled zucchini
2   tablespoons chopped onion
2   tablespoons diced bell pepper
4   tablespoons margarine
2   tablespoons parsley flakes
½   teaspoon salt
¼   teaspoon black pepper
¼   teaspoon garlic powder
¼   teaspoon dried sweet basil
¼   teaspoon dried oregano
2   eggs, well beaten
2   cups grated mozzarella cheese
1   teaspoon prepared mustard
1   (9-inch) pie shell, unbaked

Summer

Main Dishes

Fresh Tomato and Pesto Pizza

2 tablespoons olive
   oil
1 commercially
   prepared (12-
   inch) pizza crust
   or focaccia bread
¾ cup pesto
2 fresh tomatoes,
   sliced
3 cups grated
   mozzarella cheese
Parmesan cheese
   (optional)
Fresh basil leaves for
   garnish (optional)

1. Rub oil over crust. Spread pesto over crust leaving an ½-inch edge.

2. Top with tomato slices. Cover with mozzarella cheese.

3. Bake at 400° for 15 to 20 minutes or until cheese is bubbly. Sprinkle with Parmesan cheese and garnish center of pizza with basil leaves.

Yield: 1 (12-inch) pizza

Other good pizza toppings include black olives, mushrooms, goat cheese, bell peppers, and onions.

Designer Baked Catfish Fillet

 1. Coat a small broiler pan with nonstick cooking spray. Arrange fennel on pan.

2. Place fillet on fennel. Spray fillet with nonstick cooking spray. Spread breadcrumbs over entire fillet. Sprinkle with lemon pepper and paprika.

3. Bake at 350° for 20 to 30 minutes or until fish flakes easily with a fork.

Yield: 2 *servings*

Whether an angler's gift or farm-raised, catfish is presented in grand style with bronze fennel stalks.

Good accompaniments include steamed broccoli, parsleyed potatoes, baked sweet potatoes, cornbread, or spoonbread.

Variation: Place fish on a bed of fresh globe or piccolo basil and fresh oregano, or herbs of choice.

3   stalks fresh bronze
    fennel
1   large catfish fillet
Fresh breadcrumbs
½   teaspoon lemon
    pepper
½   teaspoon
    Hungarian paprika

Summer

Herbed Salmon Steaks

8 (¾-inch-thick) salmon steaks
¾ cup dry white vermouth
¾ cup olive oil
1½ tablespoons lemon juice
1 tablespoon chopped fresh thyme
1 tablespoon chopped fresh marjoram
1 tablespoon chopped fresh sage
¾ teaspoon salt
⅛ teaspoon freshly ground black pepper

1. Place salmon in 2 shallow dishes.

2. Combine vermouth and remaining 7 ingredients to make a marinade. Reserve ⅓ cup marinade.

3. Pour remaining marinade over salmon. Cover and refrigerate 60 minutes.

4. Remove salmon from pan, discarding marinade. Grill, covered, over medium-hot coals for 5 to 6 minutes on each side or until salmon flakes easily with a fork. Brush frequently while grilling with reserved marinade.

Yield: 8 servings

Poached Orange Roughy

¾ cup Chablis
1 teaspoon dried dill
1 teaspoon celery salt
1 teaspoon cracked black pepper
4 pieces orange roughy
1 lemon, thinly sliced
1 onion, thinly sliced

 1. Simmer Chablis and next 3 ingredients about 10 minutes.

2. Place orange roughy in a baking pan. Pour wine mixture over fish. Arrange lemon and onion slices on top.

3. Cover tightly with aluminum foil. Bake at 350° for 30 minutes or until fish flakes easily with a fork.

4. Serve with low-fat or no-fat mayonnaise flavored with dill.

Yield: 4 servings

For a summertime variation, chill fish when done baking. Serve cold on lettuce with lemon slices.

White Clam Sauce and Linguine

1. Drain clams, reserving 2 cups of juice. Sauté clams and garlic in oil 5 minutes.

2. Stir in reserved juice, salt, and pepper. Simmer, uncovered, 15 minutes. Mix in parsley.

3. Cook linguine according to package directions. Serve sauce warm over linguine.

Yield: 6 to 8 servings

6	(6½-ounce) cans minced clams
2	cloves garlic, minced
⅔	cup olive oil
1¼	teaspoons salt
	Black pepper to taste
⅓	cup chopped fresh parsley
1½	pounds linguine

Broiled Chicken Breast With Pesto

1. Brush chicken with lemon juice. Season with salt and pepper.

2. Place skin side down on a broiler pan. Broil about 8 inches from heat for 5 minutes.

3. Turn chicken and broil 5 minutes longer.

4. Spread pesto over chicken. Broil 5 to 10 minutes or until meat is opaque but still juicy.

Yield: 4 servings

To grill instead of broil, place seasoned chicken in microwave and cook 10 minutes. Transfer to a grill, rib side down, and cook 6 minutes. Add pesto and turn. Cook 5 to 7 minutes longer.

This dish is easy and impressive. Serve with a pasta side dish and fresh tomatoes.

4	chicken breasts with bone
3	tablespoons fresh lemon juice
¼	teaspoon salt
⅛	teaspoon black pepper
¼	cup pesto

Summer

Herbed Chicken Strips

1 ¼ cups rolled oats
1 ¼ teaspoons dried
      basil
  1   teaspoon paprika
  ½   teaspoon dried
      oregano
  ½   teaspoon dried
      thyme
  ¼   teaspoon garlic
      powder
  4   chicken breasts,
      boned and skinned
  ¼   cup milk
  4   tablespoons
      margarine, melted
  1   (8-ounce) can
      tomato sauce
  ½   cup sliced green
      onions

1. Process oats in a blender or a food processor until fine. Combine oats with basil and next 4 ingredients; set aside.

2. Cut breasts into 1-inch-wide strips. Coat chicken in oat mixture. Dip into milk and then into oat mixture again.

3. Place in a greased 15x10x1-inch pan. Drizzle with margarine.

4. Bake at 425° for 25 to 30 minutes or until tender.

5. Combine tomato sauce and onions. Serve sauce with chicken.

Yield: 4 servings

Chicken Salad

1. Cook macaroni according to package. Drain.

2. Combine macaroni with chicken and next 4 ingredients.

3. Mix sour cream and remaining 6 ingredients. Add to chicken mixture. Blend thoroughly and chill.

Yield: 4 to 6 servings

Layers of herb flavor add another reason why chicken salad is always enjoyed and never out-of-fashion.

1   cup uncooked shell macaroni
2   cups cooked and cubed chicken
1   cup chopped celery
1   cup halved seedless green grapes
½   cup salted cashews
¼   cup slivered almonds
⅓   cup sour cream
⅓   cup mayonnaise
1   tablespoon mustard-mayonnaise sauce
1   teaspoon dried tarragon
1   teaspoon dried dill
½   teaspoon dried sage
¼   teaspoon celery seed

Summer

Lemon Basil Chicken Salad

½ cup mayonnaise-
   type salad dressing
2 tablespoons
   chopped fresh
   basil, or 2
   teaspoons dried
1 tablespoon lemon
   juice
1 teaspoon lemon
   zest
2 cups chopped
   cooked chicken or
   turkey
1 cup halved red or
   green grapes
½ cup halved snow
   pea pods
½ cup thinly sliced
   red onion
½ cup pineapple
   tidbits

1. Combine salad dressing and next 3 ingredients in a large bowl.

2. Add chicken and remaining 4 ingredients.
Mix lightly. Chill.

3. Serve on lettuce leaves.

Yield: 4 servings

Nana's Chicken Salad

1. Boil chicken until tender. Remove from liquid and cool. Cut into small chunks.

2. Combine oil and garlic. Pour over chicken and let stand 30 minutes.

3. Add egg and next 7 ingredients.

4. When ready to serve, combine salt, pepper, and next 3 ingredients. Add to chicken and mix. Garnish.

Yield: 4 to 6 servings

1	(3- to 4½-pound) chicken
¼	cup olive oil
1	teaspoon minced garlic
4	hard-cooked eggs, chopped
1	dill pickle, chopped
1	bunch celery hearts, chopped
2	tablespoons sweet relish
2	teaspoons fresh lemon balm
2	teaspoons fresh tarragon
2	teaspoons fresh basil
2	teaspoons fresh onion chives
Salt and pepper to taste	
1	cup mayonnaise
1	tablespoon lemon juice
1	tablespoon tarragon vinegar
Fresh parsley and radish flowers for garnish	

Summer

Rosemary Sage Chicken

4 teaspoons fresh rosemary leaves
1 teaspoon chopped fresh sage
2 cloves garlic, minced
1 teaspoon lemon zest
¼ teaspoon black pepper
1 (3- to 4-pound) chicken
1 tablespoon lemon juice
1 tablespoon vegetable oil

1. Combine rosemary and next 4 ingredients.

2.Rinse chicken and pat dry. Sprinkle a fourth of herb mixture in chicken cavity. Brush or rub lemon juice and oil over chicken. Sprinkle remaining herb mixture evenly over chicken. Place on a rack in a foil-lined roasting pan.

3. Bake at 375° for 1 hour, 15 minutes or until tender and golden brown.

Yield: 4 to 6 servings

Beef Kebobs

2 pounds boneless beef
1 cup burgundy
1 cup rosemary red wine vinegar
½ cup olive oil
2 tablespoons dried basil
2 large cloves garlic, crushed
2 tablespoons salt
1 tablespoon black pepper
Vegetables of choice: cherry tomatoes, mushrooms, bell peppers, onions
Fresh parsley

1. Cut beef into large cubes. Combine burgundy and next 6 ingredients to make a marinade. Pour over beef. Refrigerate over-night.

2. Cut vegetables, as necessary, into large chunks. Assemble kebobs by threading skewers with beef and vegetables. Place kebobs in marinade for a few hours.

3. Remove kebobs from marinade. Grill for 5 to 6 minutes on each side. Serve on a platter. Garnish with fresh parsley.

Yield: 4 to 6 servings

Desserts

Anise Hyssop Lemon Cake

1. Prepare cake mix as directed on package.

2. Fold anise hyssop and pecans into batter. Pour batter into a greased and floured Bundt pan.

3. Bake at 350° for 35 to 40 minutes or until a toothpick inserted in the center comes out clean. Cool in pan for 10 minutes on a rack.

4. Remove cake from pan and continue cooling on rack.

Yield: 10 to 12 servings

The anise hyssop provides mint and licorice flavors.

1 (18-ounce) package lemon cake mix
1 cup chopped fresh, dried, or frozen anise hyssop flowers
1 cup chopped pecans, toasted

Lemon Sauce

1. Boil water in a saucepan. Add sugar, flour, and salt. Bring to a boil and cook 3 minutes, stirring constantly.

2. Add juice and remaining 3 ingredients.

3. Serve warm over Anise Hyssop Lemon Cake or pound cake.

Yield: about 1½ cups

1 cup water
1 cup sugar
2 tablespoons all-purpose flour
¼ teaspoon salt
3 tablespoons lemon juice
2 teaspoons lemon zest
1 tablespoon butter
1 tablespoon chopped lemon verbena

Summer

Refreshing Lemon Cake

Cake

2 (¼-ounce) envelopes plain gelatin
1 cup lemon juice
6 eggs, separated
2 cups sugar, divided
1 tablespoon lemon zest
1 angel food cake, cut into 1-inch cubes

Frosting

1 cup heavy cream
¼ cup powdered sugar
Yellow food coloring
1 tablespoon chopped fresh lemon thyme
Unsprayed rose petals or other edible flowers for garnish

1. Combine gelatin and lemon juice and let stand 5 minutes.

2. Beat egg yolks until thick and lemon colored. Combine yolk, gelatin mixture, and 1 cup sugar in a small saucepan.

3. Cook over low heat until thick. Cool. Mix in zest.

4. In a separate bowl, beat egg whites until soft peaks form. Gradually add remaining 1 cup sugar and continue beating until peaks are stiff and glossy.

5. Fold lemon mixture into egg white. Gently fold cake into mixture, coating all cubes thoroughly.

6. Spoon into a lightly greased 10-inch tube pan. Refrigerate overnight. Remove from pan.

7. To make frosting, beat together cream, sugar, and food coloring. Mix in thyme. Frost cake. Garnish when ready to serve.

Yield: 8 to 10 servings

Fresh Peaches Gratin
With Rose Geranium and Cardamom

1. Place milk and next 3 ingredients in a blender in order listed. Increasing speed while running, mix 1 to 2 seconds or until thoroughly blended. Do not overmix.

2. Pour into a small stainless steel or glass saucepan. Cook over medium heat, stirring constantly with a straight-bottomed spatula, until sauce thickens and is smooth.

3. Pour into a bowl to cool slightly. Add rose geranium, cardamom seed, and vanilla. If lumps form, cool slightly and reblend until smooth.

4. While sauce is still hot, add cheese. Mix with a wire whip until smooth. Refrigerate until needed.

5. Warm sauce to room temperature before proceeding.

6. Prepare peaches within 1 hour of baking. Peel peaches, if desired, and cut into 12 to 16 slices each. Dip in diluted lemon juice to prevent discoloration. Drain any juice from slices.

7. Place in a greased 13x9x2-inch baking dish. Sprinkle with almonds. Spoon sauce evenly over top. Sprinkle with crumbs.

8. Bake at 400° for 15 to 20 minutes or until bubbly and lightly browned. Serve hot or warm.

Yield: 6 to 8 servings

Other sweet herbs would be delicious, such as spearmint, lemon verbena, lemon balm, or even rosemary. Fruit should not be cut more than 1 hour ahead or too much juice will be lost. Gratin can also be browned under a broiler, but must be carefully watched to prevent burning.

Madalene Hill and Gwen Barclay
Copyright © 1992

2 cups whole milk or light cream
2 eggs
⅔ cup sugar
2 tablespoons cornstarch
1 tablespoon chopped fresh rose geranium
½ teaspoon freshly ground cardamom seed
1 teaspoon vanilla
½ cup whole milk ricotta cheese or cream cheese, softened
4-6 ripe peaches
Diluted lemon juice
⅓ cup sliced almonds, toasted
¼ cup plain cookie or cake crumbs

Summer

Berry Balm Crunch

16 ounces blackberries, raspberries, or blueberries
2 tablespoons lemon juice
4 tablespoons finely chopped fresh lemon balm
⅔ cup packed brown sugar
½ cup all-purpose flour
⅔ cup quick-cooking rolled oats
5 tablespoons butter, softened
1 teaspoon cinnamon
Sprigs of fresh lemon balm for garnish

1. Combine berries, lemon juice, and lemon balm. Spread in an 8-inch square baking pan.

2. Mix sugar and next 4 ingredients. Sprinkle over berries.

3. Bake at 375° for 30 minutes or until crisp and brown. Serve warm with ice cream and garnish.

Yield: 4 servings

A comfort dessert you'll enjoy serving for a summer's evening.

 For a quick-and-easy appetizer or after-dinner treat, add chopped chocolate mint to strawberry cream cheese. Serve in a small crock with gingersnaps or fresh fruit slices. It's a good idea for brunches or children's birthday parties.

Double-Your-Pleasure Pies

1. Mix together ice cream and lemonade concentrate. Divide evenly into two bowls.

2. In one bowl, mix in lemon balm. Pour into graham cracker pie crust. Freeze.

3. In second bowl, mix in chocolate mint. Pour into chocolate wafer pie crust. Freeze.

4. Garnish each serving with an appropriate fresh herb sprig.

Yield: 16 servings

½ gallon vanilla ice cream, softened

½ (6-ounce) can frozen pink lemonade concentrate, thawed

2 tablespoons finely chopped fresh lemon balm

1 (9-inch) graham cracker pie crust

2 tablespoons finely chopped fresh chocolate mint leaves

1 (9-inch) chocolate wafer pie crust

8 sprigs fresh lemon balm for garnish

8 sprigs fresh chocolate mint for garnish

Summer

Rose Geranium Buttermilk Pound Cake

2   sticks margarine
2¾   cups sugar
4   eggs
2   teaspoons vanilla
1   tablespoon lemon zest
Pinch of salt
½   cup finely minced fresh rose geranium leaves
3   cups all-purpose flour
¼   teaspoon baking soda
1   cup buttermilk
6   whole fresh rose geranium leaves
Powdered sugar for topping

1. Using an electric mixer, cream margarine and sugar until fluffy.

2. Beat in eggs one at a time. Mix well.

3. On slow speed, add vanilla and next 3 ingredients.

4. In a separate bowl, combine flour and baking soda. To the batter, add dry ingredients in 3 portions and buttermilk in 2 portions, alternating between the two. Mix well to moisten flour.

5. Place whole rose geranium leaves in the bottom of a greased and floured Bundt pan. Carefully pour batter into pan.

6. Bake at 325° for exactly 1 hour, 10 minutes, even if cake does not appear done at end of cooking time. Cool for 10 minutes. Remove from pan. Dust with powdered sugar.

Yield: 10 to 12 servings

This cake freezes well. Replace lemon zest with 2 teaspoons lemon extract and 1 teaspoon vanilla, if needed.

Lavender Faerie Cookies

1. Cream butter and sugar. Beat in eggs, vanilla, and lavender flowers. Stir in flour and baking powder until well blended.

2. Drop by half teaspoons on an ungreased baking sheet.

3. Bake at 375° for 6 to 8 minutes. Cool slightly on baking sheet before transferring to a cooling rack.

Yield: 3 to 4 dozen

1   stick butter
1   cup sugar
2   eggs
½   teaspoon vanilla
1   tablespoon finely chopped fresh lavender flowers
1½ cups all-purpose flour
2   teaspoons baking powder

Nepali Melon Sherbet

1. Place all ingredients in blender and liquefy, adding water if needed.

2. Pour mixture into sherbet glasses and refrigerate until serving time.

Yield: 6 to 8 servings

4   cups diced melon of choice
1   tablespoon yogurt
1   tablespoon sugar
1   tablespoon fresh mint leaves, or more to taste

Herbs Butters

Herbs blended into unsalted butter or margarine is one of the easiest and most satisfying uses for herbs. Anywhere you would dab butter, herb butter will do fine: sauces, soups, gravies, pasta and rice dishes, and vegetables. Dab a bit on poached fish or grilled or broiled meat.

Herb butters can be shaped or pressed for gifts, as well as easily stored in the freezer to use as needed.

Method: Unsalted butter is preferred because it allows for the fullest herb flavor. While it softens, rinse herbs and pat or spin dry before chopping, snipping, or crushing. For dried herbs, pulverize with a mortar and pestle.

Flavor tips: Parsley enhances the flavor of all herbs. Parmesan cheese and nuts are good with many herbs. Add small amounts of garlic, Dijon mustard, dry mustard, curry powder, celery seed, hot pepper sauce, paprika, orange or lemon zest, green onions.

Good herb and butter combinations: • dill, mustard, parsley; • sage, parsley, chives; • tarragon, fennel, parsley, lemon zest; • salad burnet, garlic chives, parsley • savory, marjoram, parsley; • Fines herbes butter: chives, parsley, tarragon, chervil

Savory Herb Butter

1 cup unsalted butter or margarine
3 tablespoons fresh chopped herbs or
   3 teaspoons dried herbs
1 tablespoon lemon juice
Salt and pepper to taste

With a spoon, blend herbs into softened butter. Refrigerate overnight for flavors to mix. Taste the next day. Add more herbs for additional flavor. If flavors are too strong, stir in more butter.

Makes 1 ¼ cups or 20 tablespoons

Sweet Herb Butter

An unexpected delight with croissants, sweet breads, pancakes, waffles, and muffins

1 cup unsalted butter or margarine
4 tablespoons fresh sweet-scented
   herbs: scented geranium leaves,
   lemon balm, lemon verbena and
   mints: orange, grapefruit, or lemon
½ teaspoon orange zest
2 tablespoons pureed or finely
   chopped fruits (strawberries,
   raspberries, peaches)
1 tablespoon fruit liqueur
2 tablespoons chopped nuts

Chop herbs and blend all ingredients into softened butter. Refrigerate overnight. Taste in morning and make adjustments, as desired.

Makes 1 ½ cups or 25 tablespoons

Herbs in Autumn

The transition from school vacations, family holidays, and lazy days is as brisk as autumn air. Appetites rise to the change of activity pace, and everyone welcomes soups and stews and other hearty meals made with herbs. Revel in the harvest, and anticipate the holidays by preparing herb vinegars, ornamental bouquets, and dried herb mixes.

Herbs in Autumn

Line drawers and linen shelves with dried lavender.

Sage is the dominant herb in poultry seasoning used to make many a Thanksgiving turkey stuffing.

Add a teaspoon of anise or caraway seeds, dill, marjoram, oregano, basil, or thyme to basic yeast breads or those made in bread machines. Your home will smell cozy and feel warm during this cool season.

Add caraway seeds to apple pie filling.

Appetizers, Beverages, Etc.

Cheesy Salmon Ball

1. Cook bacon until crisp. Drain and crumble.

2. Drain and flake salmon.

3. Combine bacon, salmon, and next 7 ingredients. Mix well.

4. Form into a ball and refrigerate overnight. Roll in finely chopped fresh parsley to garnish.

Yield: 8 to 10 servings

6   slices bacon
1   (14½-ounce) can pink salmon, or fresh, cooked
1   (8-ounce) package fat-free cream cheese
1   cup grated sharp Cheddar cheese
½   cup chopped Spanish olives
3   tablespoons minced onion
2   dashes hot pepper sauce
⅓   cup finely chopped fresh parsley
⅓   cup chopped fresh rosemary
    Parsley for garnish

Texas Caviar

2 (16-ounce) cans black-eyed peas, rinsed and drained
2 large tomatoes, seeded and finely chopped
½ cup chopped fresh cilantro
½ cup chopped onion
¼ cup chopped fresh basil
¼ cup chopped fresh parsley
2 jalapeño peppers, seeded, deveined, and chopped
1 clove garlic, chopped
¼ cup white wine vinegar
Salt and freshly ground pepper to taste

1. Mix all ingredients well and chill overnight.

2. Serve with tortilla chips.

Yield: 8 servings

Turn to the garden instead of the sea for this interpretation of caviar.

Applemint Wreaths

Form wreaths with long stems of mint with seed heads. Tie with a red ribbon and an apple card with instructions for planting seeds. Add jellies and teabags in the center.

Apple or Pear Chutney

1. Combine apples and next 8 ingredients in a large pot. Simmer 2 hours or until thick. Monitor closely during cooking time to prevent burning. Add extra water, if necessary.

2. Add pectin and simmer 5 minutes. Mix in cloves and remaining 4 ingredients. Boil 1 minute, stirring constantly. Remove bay leaves.

3. Place mixture in sterilized jars and seal. Refrigerate after opening.

Yield: 6 to 8 pints

Use with curried meats, poultry, or fish, or mix with cream cheese to make a dip.

You'll be rewarded for preserving the harvest when there's a spicy chutney simmering on the range top. Also, chutney is delicious stirred into cream cheese as a cracker spread.

5	pounds apples or pears, finely chopped
1	(16-ounce) can crushed pineapple
1	large bell pepper, seeded and chopped
1½	cups raisins
1	cup crystallized ginger, chopped
4	cups sugar
3	cups vinegar
½	teaspoon salt
1	cup water
1	(3-ounce) envelope liquid pectin
¼	teaspoon ground cloves
½	teaspoon cinnamon
¼	teaspoon nutmeg
¼	teaspoon ground allspice
6	dried bay leaves

Autumn

Aïoli Sauce I

1 cup olive oil, divided
5 large cloves garlic, peeled
3 egg yolks, or 6 tablespoons egg substitute
3 tablespoons lemon juice

1. Mix ¼ cup oil and next 3 ingredients in a blender, at low speed, until smooth. Continue to blend while gradually adding remaining ¾ cup oil.

2. Serve at room temperature, refrigerate, or freeze. Serve on bread or add to soups and vegetables.

Yield: about 1¼ cups

Aïoli Sauce II

1¼ cup mayonnaise, divided
6 cloves garlic, peeled
2 tablespoons fresh lemon juice

1. Combine ¼ cup mayonnaise, garlic, and lemon juice in a food processor and blend thoroughly. Transfer mixture to a bowl.

2. Mix in remaining 1 cup mayonnaise. Refrigerate until ready to serve.

3. Serve on fish or as a dip for raw vegetables.

Yield: about 1¼ cups

Herb or Erb—what's the difference?
Well, either is correct, but you're more likely to hear "herb" in Great Britain and "erb" in the United States.

Lemon Verbena Jelly

1. Combine lemon verbena and water in a saucepan. Bring to a boil. Remove from heat, cover, and cool.

2. Strain juice. Measure 3 cups of strained liquid into a large kettle. Add vinegar and next 3 ingredients. Stir well to dissolve.

3. Bring mixture to a boil. Boil 1 minute. Add sugar and stir well to dissolve. Add butter. Slowly bring to a boil, stirring constantly. Boil 1 minute. Remove from heat.

4. Ladle into 4- or 8-ounce sterilized jars, filling 1/8-inch to 1/4-inch from top. Stir 2 or 3 lemon verbena sprigs into each jar. Wipe rims and seal. Process in a boiling-water bath for 5 minutes.

5. Remove from water, cover jars with a towel, and let stand overnight.

Yield: 4 or 5 half-pints

3   cups torn fresh lemon verbena leaves
3¾ cups water
¼   cup cider vinegar
2   drops yellow food coloring (optional)
¼   cup lemon powder
1   (1.75-ounce) package fruit pectin
4   cups sugar
1   tablespoon butter
Sprigs of fresh lemon verbena for jars

Hot Apple Cider

1. Combine all ingredients in a large electric coffee pot. Heat.

2. Before serving, remove spices.

Yield: 1 gallon

8   whole allspice
8   whole cloves
8   whole cinnamon sticks
1   gallon apple cider
¼   cup sugar (if cider is unsweetened)
1   lemon, thinly sliced
½   orange, thinly sliced

Autumn

Herb Sticks

1 (8-count) package
day-old hot dog
buns
2 sticks margarine,
softened
1 teaspoon dried
rosemary
1 teaspoon dried
thyme
1 teaspoon dried
parsley
1 teaspoon lemon
zest
Garlic powder
(optional)

1. Cut off round ends of each bun and split in half. Cut each piece lengthwise for a total of 32 breadsticks.

2. Combine margarine and remaining 5 ingredients. Spread mixture over each breadstick.

3. Place on a baking sheet. Bake at 300° for 30 minutes or until baked to desired crispness.

4. Serve with a green salad and herbal tea.

Yield: 32 breadsticks

Bookmarkers

Place pressed herbs on a strip of plastic. Cover with contact paper. Punch hole in top and add small piece of ribbon and you have a bookmark. Include one when you give this book to a friend.

Herbal Cornbread

1. Sift together flour and next 3 ingredients. Stir in cornmeal.

2. Add eggs, milk, and oil. Beat until just smooth. Stir in onion.

3. Preheat a skillet in a 425° oven. Grease sides and bottom of hot skillet. Sprinkle with rosemary. Add batter.

4. Bake at 425° for 20 to 25 minutes. Drizzle with honey while cooling.

Yield: 4 to 6 servings

1 cup all-purpose flour
¼ cup sugar
4 teaspoons baking powder
¾ teaspoon salt
1 cup yellow cornmeal
2 eggs
1 cup milk
¼ cup oil
1 medium-size yellow onion, finely diced
1 tablespoon rosemary
2 tablespoons honey (optional)

Moth-Repellent Sachet

1 cup rosemary
1 cup vetiver
1 cup pennyroyal
5 whole bruised bay leaves

Mix all ingredients together, and tie into cheesecloth bags. Place among clothes in drawers or closets.

Autumn

Mexican Cornbread

1½ cups cornmeal
2 teaspoons baking powder
½ teaspoon salt
½ cup chopped onion
2 jalapeño peppers, seeded and chopped
1 cup grated sharp Cheddar cheese
2 eggs
1 cup sour cream
½ cup vegetable oil
1 (17-ounce) can cream-style corn

1. Mix all ingredients together. Pour into a 9x9-inch pan.

2. Bake at 350° for 30 minutes or until golden brown and a toothpick inserted near the center comes out clean.

Yield: 4 to 6 servings

Omit baking powder if using self-rising cornmeal.

Mint Yogurt Bread

1 (¼-ounce) package active dry yeast
⅓ cup warm water
1 cup plain yogurt
3 cups bread flour
3 tablespoons chopped fresh mint
Zest of 1 lemon
2 teaspoons honey
1 teaspoon butter, softened

1. Combine yeast and water. Let stand a few minutes until bubbly.

2. Add yogurt and remaining 5 ingredients. Knead until smooth.

3. Place in a greased bowl and cover with plastic wrap. Let rise until doubled in size.

4. Transfer to 1 large or 2 small loaf pans.

5. Bake at 350° for about 20 minutes. Lower heat to 325° and bake 10 minutes or until golden brown.

Yield: 1 large loaf or 2 small loaves

Oatmeal Bread With Rosemary and Walnuts

1. Combine oats and oil in a bowl. Boil water and pour over oat mixture.

2. Stir in honey and salt. Cool until warm.

3. Combine yeast, 6 cups flour, and rosemary. Add warm oat mixture. Blend well. Add walnuts.

4. Mix in remaining flour as needed. Turn onto a floured surface and knead until smooth. Add extra flour if necessary.

5. Place dough in a lightly greased bowl and cover. Let rise 1 hour, 30 minutes to 2 hours or until doubled in size. Punch down dough.

6. Form into 3 large or 6 small loaves and place in greased loaf pans. Cover and let rise until dough reaches top of pan or until doubled.

7. Bake at 350° for 20 minutes. Lower heat to 300° or 325° and bake 20 minutes longer or until done. Let cool in pan for 5 minutes. Remove from pan and cool on a rack.

Yield: 3 large or 6 small loaves

1½ cups rolled oats
3 tablespoons walnut oil
3 cups water
1 cup honey
1½ teaspoons salt
2 (¼-ounce) packages active dry yeast
6½-7 cups all-purpose flour, divided
2 tablespoons chopped dried rosemary
1½ cups coarsely chopped walnuts

Autumn

Rose Geranium Scones

2¼ cups all-purpose flour
6-7 tablespoons sugar
4 teaspoons baking powder
½ teaspoon salt
6 tablespoons cold butter, cut in small pieces
1 cup loosely packed, chopped fresh rose geranium leaves
1 (5-ounce) can evaporated milk
2 eggs, well beaten
Cornmeal

1. Combine flour and next 3 ingredients. Cut in butter until crumbly. Add rose geranium.

2. Mix together milk and egg thoroughly. Reserve 1 to 2 tablespoons of milk mixture. Add remainder to flour mixture and blend until just mixed. Do not overbeat.

3. Turn dough onto a floured surface. Form into a ball. Flatten with a rolling pin to ½-inch thick. Cut into 3-inch squares. Cut each square into 2 triangles.

4. Sprinkle cornmeal on a nonstick baking sheet. Place 4 triangles on sheet, leaving an ½-inch space between them. Brush with reserved milk mixture. Sprinkle with extra sugar.

5. Bake at 425° for 10 to 15 minutes or until lightly browned. Remove from sheet and cool until warm. Serve with butter or herb jelly. Cool leftovers thoroughly and store in a plastic bag. Reheat before serving.

Yield: about 3 dozen

These are delicious for an afternoon tea or a festive breakfast or brunch.

Rosemary Soda Bread

1. Sift together whole wheat flour and next 7 ingredients. Stir in sunflower seed.

2. Combine egg, buttermilk, and butter. Mix into dry ingredients. Knead lightly in bowl. Form into a ball.

3. Place on a greased baking sheet and flatten slightly.

4. Bake at 350° for 30 to 40 minutes. Cool slightly and cut into thin slices.

Yield: 1 loaf

⅔ cup whole wheat flour

⅓ cup soy flour

1 cup unbleached all-purpose flour

1½ teaspoons baking powder

½ teaspoon baking soda

½ teaspoon salt

1 teaspoon powdered rosemary

3 tablespoons sugar

¼ cup sunflower seed

1 egg, lightly beaten

⅔ cup buttermilk

1 tablespoon butter, melted

During autumn, take a walk in the garden or the woods looking for such decorative complements for herb bouquets as bittersweet, cattails, and milkweed pods. Take care not to uproot live plants. Leave plants to regenerate for seasons to come.

Autumn

Sesame Tarragon Wafers

1 stick butter, softened
1 cup packed brown sugar
1 teaspoon vanilla
1 egg
½ cup sesame seed, toasted
½ cup crushed pecans or walnuts
1½ teaspoons pulverized tarragon
¾ cup all-purpose flour
¼ teaspoon baking powder
¼ teaspoon salt

1. Cream butter, brown sugar, and vanilla. Beat in egg. Stir in sesame seed, pecans, and tarragon.

2. Sift together flour, baking powder, and salt. Add dry ingredients to creamed mixture. Mix well.

3. Drop in small mounds, about 3 inches apart, onto a greased baking sheet.

4. Bake at 375° for 8 to 10 minutes. Cool 1 minute before removing from baking sheet.

Yield: 4 dozen wafers

Variation: To make Tarragon Wafers, omit the sesame seeds.

A sweet cookie joined with sesame and tarragon. Serve with dessert wine or brewed tea.

Spiral Bread

1. In a large bowl, combine 2½ cups flour and next 3 ingredients. Heat water, milk, and butter until very warm, 120° to 130°. Slowly add liquid mixture to dry ingredients. Beat with an electric mixer on medium speed for 2 minutes.

2. Add ½ cup flour and beat on high speed for 2 minutes. With a spoon, stir in enough of remaining flour to form a soft dough. Knead on a lightly floured surface 8 to 10 minutes or until smooth and elastic.

3. Place dough in a greased bowl, turning dough to grease top. Cover. Let rise in a warm, draft-free place 30 to 60 minutes or until doubled in size. Punch dough down and turn out of bowl. Let stand 10 minutes.

4. To make filling, sauté parsley, green onion, and garlic in butter over medium heat. Cook, stirring often, until onion appears translucent, but not browned. Mixture should reduce to about half its volume. Cool.

5. Add salt, hot pepper sauce, and black pepper. Reserve egg and melted butter for brushing over dough. Cut dough in half. Roll each half into a rectangle about ½ inch thick and 9 inches wide. Brush dough with reserved egg.

6. Spread filling over dough to 1 inch from edge. Roll from narrow end and pinch edges to seal. Place in 2 greased 9x5x3-inch loaf pans. Brush top of dough with reserved melted butter.

7. Cover and let rise in a warm, draft-free place 50 to 60 minutes or until higher in the middle than at the edge of pan. Cut gashes in top of loaves, if desired.

8. Bake at 400° for 60 minutes. Remove from pans and cool on a rack.

Yield: 2 loaves

Dough

6-6½	cups all-purpose flour, divided
3	tablespoons sugar
2	(¼-ounce) packages active dry yeast, regular or quick-rising
2	teaspoons salt
1½	cups water
½	cup milk
2	tablespoons butter or margarine

Green Herb Filling

2	cups finely chopped fresh parsley
2	cups finely chopped green onion
1	large clove garlic, minced
2	tablespoons butter
¾	teaspoon salt
	Hot pepper sauce to taste
	Freshly ground black pepper to taste
2	eggs, lightly beaten
	Melted butter or salad oil

Autumn

Soups, Sandwiches, Salads

Four-minute Tomato Bisque

1 (10¾-ounce) can condensed cream of tomato soup
1 pint half-and-half or whole milk
½ teaspoon crumbled dried basil, or 2 teaspoons fresh
1 teaspoon dried minced onion
1 teaspoon sugar
1 tablespoons chopped fresh chives
Croutons

1. Combine soup and next 4 ingredients in a 1½-quart saucepan. Slowly heat to just boiling. Reduce heat and simmer 2 minutes, stirring constantly.

2. Top each serving with chives and croutons.

Yield: 4 servings

Mix chopped parsley with a little grated lemon peel to garnish soups and stews.

October Bisque

1. Sauté onion in butter until tender. Add broth and simmer 15 minutes.

2. Process tomatoes in a blender or food processor until smooth. Add tomato and remaining ingredients to broth. Heat to serve.

Yield: 8 to 10 servings

1 large onion, chopped
4 tablespoons butter
4 cups chicken broth
1 (28-ounce) can whole tomatoes, undrained
1 tablespoon sugar
2 (16-ounce) cans pumpkin, or 4 cups pureed fresh
2 tablespoons chopped fresh parsley
2 tablespoons chopped fresh chives
Salt and pepper to taste

Roman legions brought thyme to England where ladies took to weaving sprigs of thyme into their knights' scarves to remind them to be brave.

Autumn

Southern Soup

3   leeks, thinly sliced
2   tablespoons olive oil or herbed oil
2   medium sweet potatoes, peeled and cubed
3   (14-ounce) cans chicken broth
4   cups shredded cooked chicken
1   teaspoon dried thyme, or 2 teaspoons fresh
⅛   teaspoon black pepper
2   bunches kale, stemmed and cut into thin strips

1. In a large saucepan, sauté leeks in oil for 2 minutes. Add sweet potato and broth. Cover and bring to a boil. Boil 2 minutes.

2. Reduce heat and simmer 15 minutes or until potato is tender. Add chicken, thyme, and pepper. Continue to simmer.

3. Add kale a few minutes before ready to serve. Cook 5 minutes or until kale wilts and is soft.

Yield: 6 servings

This recipe makes use of sweet potatoes, kale, and leftover chicken to turn ordinary broth into a sensation.

This dish is a nutrient bonanza with the added asset of being low in fat.

Table Decoration

Glue empty herb seed packets around a small clay pot and put a votive candle inside. Group pots for table decorations.

Cornbread Turkey Sandwiches

1. In a small skillet, cook curry powder over medium heat for 1 minute or until very fragrant. While cooking, stir constantly with a metal spatula. Scrape into a bowl to cool.

2. Mix in mayonnaise and next 3 ingredients.

3. To assemble sandwiches, cut cornbread into wedges or squares. Slice in half. Cover lower half with a generous amount of curry apple mayonnaise. Top with turkey. Spread 1 tablespoon of cranberry sauce over turkey. Cover with other half of cornbread. Serve immediately.

Yield: 4 to 6 servings

This recipe adds a different twist to turkey sandwiches made from Thanksgiving leftovers.

Curry Apple Mayonnaise

- 2 teaspoons curry powder
- ¾ cup mayonnaise
- 1 large tart apple, peeled and finely diced
- 2 teaspoons freshly squeezed lemon juice
- Salt to taste

Sandwiches

- 1 pan cornbread
- Curry apple mayonnaise
- 1 pound cooked turkey
- 1 can whole-berry cranberry sauce

Sage and Cheddar Cheese Melties

1. Combine cheese and sage. Mix well. Spread bread slices lightly with mayonnaise. Sprinkle cheese mixture evenly over slices.

2. Cut each slice into 4 triangles. Arrange on 2 baking sheets. Preheat broiler. In 2 batches, broil sandwiches 3 inches from heat for 1 minute or until cheese melts and starts to brown.

3. Garnish each sandwich. Serve immediately.

Yield: 48 sandwiches

- 1 cup grated Cheddar cheese
- ¼ cup chopped fresh sage
- 12 thin slices wheat or white bread, crusts removed
- Mayonnaise
- Fresh sage blossoms or leaves for garnish

Autumn

Grilled Sandwiches

8 slices bacon
Butter or margarine,
   softened
8 slices sandwich
   bread
4 slices mozzarella
   cheese
⅓ cup sour cream
2 tablespoons
   chopped onion
Fresh or dried
   oregano
2 tomatoes, sliced
Seasoned salt

1. Cook bacon until crisp. Drain. Spread butter on both sides of bread slices.

2. Assemble sandwiches by topping 4 slices of bread with a slice of cheese and a dollop of sour cream. Divide onion evenly over sandwiches and sprinkle with oregano. Distribute tomato slices between sandwiches and sprinkle with seasoned salt. Top each sandwich with 2 slices of bacon and another slice of bread.

3. Place sandwiches, cheese side down, in a skillet. Cover and cook until bread browns and cheese melts. Turn and brown other side, uncovered.

Yield: 4 sandwiches

An electric skillet set at about 350i works well for browning the sandwiches.

With a sprinkle of fresh or dried oregano, this cheese sandwich becomes a special lunch for an ordinary day.

Wild Rice Chicken Salad

1. Rinse rice. Combine rice and next 3 ingredients in a saucepan. Bring to a boil. Cover and reduce heat. Simmer 45 minutes or until rice kernels have opened and are tender. Drain any excess liquid.

2. Sprinkle ½ teaspoon tarragon over chicken breasts and bake until done. Cool chicken and chop.

3. Mix rice, chicken, green onions, and water chestnuts in a large bowl. Combine mayonnaise, lemon juice, and remaining ½ teaspoon tarragon. Pour over rice mixture and blend thoroughly.

4. Cover and refrigerate until chilled. Fold in grapes and almonds just before serving. Add salt and pepper.

Yield: 4 to 6 servings

1	cup wild rice
1	teaspoon salt
2	cups chicken broth
2	cups water
1	teaspoon dried tarragon, divided
3	chicken breasts
½	cup chopped green onions, or to taste
1	(8-ounce) can sliced water chestnuts, drained
½	cup mayonnaise
1½	teaspoons lemon juice, or ¾ teaspoon lemon powder
1½	cups halved green grapes
½	cup almonds, toasted (optional)
	Salt and pepper to taste

For a delightful fall tea break, steep five sage leaves in a teapot of hot water; add warm honey blended with sage.

Autumn

Side Dishes

Italian Broccoli Casserole

2 (10-ounce) packages frozen cut broccoli
2 eggs, beaten
1 (11-ounce) can condensed Cheddar cheese soup
½ teaspoon dried oregano
1 (14½-ounce) can Italian-style stewed tomatoes
3 tablespoons Parmesan cheese

1. Cook broccoli in unsalted boiling water for 5 to 7 minutes. Drain well.

2. Combine egg, soup, and oregano in a bowl. Stir in broccoli and tomatoes.

3. Pour mixture into a baking dish. Sprinkle cheese over the top. Bake uncovered at 350° for 30 minutes.

Yield: 6 to 8 servings

Broccoli and Cauliflower Rice Casserole

1. Combine all ingredients. Pour into a greased casserole dish.

2. Bake uncovered at 350° for 60 minutes or until rice is tender.

Yield: 16 servings

Prepare this dish ahead and refrigerate until ready to bake. Reduce fat content by using low-fat soups and by coating casserole dish with nonstick cooking spray.

1 cup uncooked long-grain rice

1 stick butter or margarine, melted

1 (10¾-ounce) can condensed cream of mushroom soup

1 (10¾-ounce) can condensed cream of celery soup

1 cup chopped onion

1 cup chopped celery

1 (16-ounce) package frozen chopped broccoli

1 (10-ounce) package frozen cauliflower, or 2 cups blanched fresh

1 teaspoon herbes de Provence

1 (8-ounce) jar pasteurized processed cheese spread

1 cup skim milk

Autumn

Chestnut Dressing

1½ pounds chestnuts
1 stick margarine
2 large yellow onions, chopped
2 cups chopped celery with leaves
1 cup diced carrots
3 tablespoons chopped fresh sage, or 1 tablespoon dried
2 teaspoons chopped fresh thyme, or ¾ teaspoon dried
1 teaspoon chopped fresh savory, or ½ teaspoon dried
1 tablespoon fresh sweet marjoram, or 1 teaspoon dried
1 tablespoon chopped fresh rosemary, or 1 teaspoon dried
2 chicken bouillon cubes
1 cup hot water
Salt and freshly ground black pepper to taste
1 (8-ounce) bag herbed stuffing mix
1 (7-ounce) can mushroom stems and pieces, drained
1 egg
½ cup chopped fresh parsley

1. Prepare chestnuts by cutting a slit on the flat side of each nut. Place in a saucepan, cover with water, and bring to a boil. Reduce heat and simmer 20 to 30 minutes or until cooked.

2. Remove chestnuts about 12 at a time with a slotted spoon. Peel off outer shells and inner skins. Break into pieces about ½ to 1 inch in size.

3. Melt margarine in a heavy saucepan. Add onion, celery, and carrot. Cover and cook over low heat for about 5 minutes.

4. Add sage and next 4 ingredients. Combine bouillon and water and add to saucepan. Cook about 5 minutes.

5. Remove from heat and cool about 10 minutes. Add salt and pepper.

6. Transfer to a large bowl. Mix in chestnuts, stuffing mix, and mushrooms. Blend in egg. Add parsley and mix. Store in refrigerator until ready to use.

7. Stuff into a 14- to 16-pound turkey just before baking. If stuffing a smaller bird, bake extra stuffing separately for about 30 minutes.

Yield: enough to stuff a 14- to 16-pound turkey

Buy chestnuts during months they are available and prepare them as described above. Place in storage bags and freeze.

Dilled Carrots

1. Peel carrots and cut into thin slices or sticks about 3 inches long. Boil in salted water for 2 to 3 minutes. Drain.

2. Melt margarine in a saucepan. Add carrots, broth, and cream. Cook until mixture begins to thicken.

3. Add dill, salt, and pepper. Mix well.

Yield: 6 to 8 servings

6	large carrots
3	tablespoons margarine
4	tablespoons chicken broth
6	tablespoons cream
2	tablespoons chopped fresh dill
	Salt and pepper to taste

Never-Fail Carrot Ring

1. Mix all ingredients together. Place in a greased ring-shaped mold.

2. Bake at 350° for 60 minutes. Unmold onto a serving plate.

Yield: 6 to 8 servings

Fill center of ring with fresh green peas seasoned with mint leaves.

2	cups grated carrots
2	cups cottage cheese
2	cups breadcrumbs
2	eggs
½	teaspoon dry mustard
2	tablespoons minced fresh garlic chives
¼	cup grated onion
	Salt and pepper to taste

Autumn

Seattle Carrots

1 pound carrots,
    peeled
2 cloves garlic,
    chopped
½ cup olive oil
Fresh or dried
    oregano to taste
Salt to taste

 1. Cook carrots until tender. Cut into fine strips.

2. Toss carrots with garlic and oil. Add oregano and salt.

3. Serve cold or at room temperature.

Yield: 4 servings

Thyme is an acceptable substitution for oregano.

Serve along with other vegetables, or chop into green salad.

Deviled Corn

1 onion, chopped
1 bell pepper,
    chopped
1 tablespoon butter
3 tablespoons water
2 eggs, beaten
2 tablespoons
    cornstarch
2 teaspoons
    prepared mustard
2 teaspoons
    horseradish sauce
2 (17-ounce) cans
    cream-style corn
Breadcrumbs, broken
    tortilla chips, or
    crushed corn
    flakes for topping

1. Combine onion and next 3 ingredients in a small skillet. Cover and simmer until water evaporates.

2. Combine mixture with egg and next 4 ingredients in a casserole dish. Sprinkle with topping of choice.

3. Bake at 350° for 60 minutes or until slightly firm.

Yield: 8 servings

Slightly Slim Corn Pudding

1. Blend margarine and next 3 ingredients. Mix in egg and egg white. Stir in corn and remaining 3 ingredients.

2. Grease a 2-quart casserole dish with nonstick cooking spray. Pour mixture into dish.

3. Bake at 325° for 45 minutes, stirring halfway through cooking time. When done, pudding is golden brown and a knife inserted near the center comes out clean.

Yield: 6 servings

This is a good side dish to accompany a holiday turkey or ham.

Fresh chives and parsley are a flavor secret to this lighter version of scalloped corn.

1   tablespoon margarine, melted
2   tablespoons sugar
2   tablespoons all-purpose flour
1   teaspoon salt
2   eggs, beaten
2   egg whites, beaten
1   (15¼-ounce) can corn, drained, or 2 cups fresh
1¾ cups skim milk
1   tablespoon chopped fresh parsley
1   tablespoon chopped fresh chives

Bouquets garnis are small bundles of herbs and spices used as flavoring in soups, stews, and sauces. The bundles usually include parsley, thyme, and bay—with the occasional addition of peppercorns, allspice, cloves, celery leaves, tarragon, or marjoram. Make bouquet garnis ahead in cheesecloth bundles and freeze them; add frozen bundles directly to simmering mixtures.

Autumn

Eggplant Cornbread Casserole

2 medium to large
  eggplants, peeled
  and cubed
1 bell pepper, diced
½ cup chopped
  celery
1 cup chopped
  onion
2 tomatoes, diced
¾ teaspoon salt
⅛ teaspoon freshly
  ground black
  pepper
1 teaspoon Italian
  herbs
2 eggs, lightly beaten
Dash of hot pepper
  sauce
4 tablespoons
  margarine, melted
1 (8-ounce) package
  corn muffin mix

1. Cook eggplant in lightly salted water until tender. Drain well. Store in refrigerator until ready to use.

2. To prepare casserole, put eggplant and juices from storage container in a mixing bowl. Add bell pepper and remaining 10 ingredients in order listed, stirring after each addition.

3. After adding all ingredients, mix well and pour into a greased 10x10-inch or 13x9x2-inch pan.

4. Bake at 375° for 50 to 60 minutes or until golden brown.

Yield: 16 servings

Refrigerate leftovers and reheat before serving. Make an eggplant casserole by omitting the corn muffin mix.

A variation on the vegetable classic, ratatouille. Serve with grilled or roasted meats and glasses of red wine.

Mexican Eggplant

1. Peel eggplant and cut into ½-inch slices. Sprinkle sides of slices with salt and refrigerate 30 to 60 minutes. Dry slices with a paper towel. Brush sides with oil and place on a baking sheet.

2. Bake at 450° for 30 minutes. Combine chiles and next 4 ingredients in a medium saucepan. Bring to a boil over medium heat. Reduce heat and simmer 15 minutes.

3. Place eggplant in a lightly greased casserole dish. Top with half of tomato mixture and 1 cup cheese. Sprinkle with breadcrumbs. Spread remainder of tomato sauce over breadcrumbs. Top with remaining 1 cup cheese.

4. Bake at 350° for 20 minutes.

Yield: 4 to 6 servings

1   medium eggplant
Salt
Olive oil
1   (4-ounce) can chopped green chiles, undrained
1   (4-ounce) can sliced ripe olives, drained
1   (15-ounce) can tomato sauce
½   teaspoon ground cumin
¼   teaspoon garlic powder
2   cups grated Cheddar cheese, divided
½   cup breadcrumbs

Spiced Jewelry

Soften spices, such as nutmeg halves, cloves, cinnamon sticks, or star anise in warm water. Drill holes through them, and string for a necklace. Use the star anise as a centerpiece for the middle of the necklace.

Autumn

Fried Herb Potatoes

5   medium potatoes
5   tablespoons butter
    or margarine
2¼ teaspoons chopped
    fresh oregano
2½ tablespoons
    chopped fresh
    parsley
2½ tablespoons finely
    chopped celery
2½ tablespoons
    chopped onion
    Salt and pepper to
    taste

1. Cut potatoes into ⅛-inch slices. Melt butter in a heavy skillet. Add potato slices and cover.

2. Cook over medium heat about 15 minutes. Turn slices carefully using a spatula. Cook uncovered 10 to 15 minutes, turning occasionally to brown all sides.

3. During the final 5 minutes of cooking, add oregano and remaining ingredients.

Yield: 6 to 8 servings

Herb-Roasted Potatoes

2   baking potatoes
1   teaspoon dried
    tarragon, or 2
    teaspoons fresh
2   cloves garlic,
    minced
¼   teaspoon paprika
¼   teaspoon cayenne
    pepper
1   tablespoon Dijon
    mustard
1   tablespoon olive
    oil

1. Cut potatoes into 1-inch cubes.

2. Mix together tarragon and remaining 5 ingredients. Toss seasoning mixture with potato.

3. Place on baking sheet and bake at 425° for 30 minutes or until tender.

Yield: 2 to 4 servings

Potato Gratin With Basil

1. In a large skillet, sauté onion in 2 tablespoons oil until tender. Add bell pepper and sauté 3 minutes. Add tomato and cook and stir until excess moisture evaporates. Add salt and pepper and next 3 ingredients and cook 1 minute.

2. Cut potatoes into ¼-inch slices. Spread half of potato in a casserole dish. Arrange half of vegetable mixture on top and sprinkle with ¼ cup Monterey Jack cheese. Repeat layers of potato, vegetable mixture, and cheese. Drizzle remaining 1 tablespoon oil over top and cover tightly with foil.

3. Bake at 400° for 30 minutes. Remove foil and sprinkle with Parmesan cheese. Continue baking, uncovered, for 15 minutes or until potatoes are tender and top is brown. Garnish.

Yield: 8 to 10 servings

Substitute a different cheese for Monterey Jack, if desired.

1   onion, sliced
3   tablespoons olive oil, divided
1   red bell pepper, seeded and sliced
1   ripe tomato, peeled, seeded, and chopped
Salt and pepper to taste
2   cloves garlic, minced
¼   teaspoon crushed red pepper flakes
2   tablespoons chopped fresh basil
6   baking potatoes
½   cup grated Monterey Jack cheese, divided
¼   cup Parmesan cheese
Fresh basil for garnish

Cinnamon and clove oils are powerful germicides.

Autumn

Rice With Pine Nuts

3 tablespoons butter, divided
¼ cup chopped onion
¼ cup pine nuts
Salt and freshly ground pepper to taste
1 cup converted rice
1¼ cups water
2 sprigs fresh thyme, or ½ teaspoon dried
1 dried bay leaf

1. Melt 2 tablespoons butter in an oven-safe saucepan. Add onion and nuts and cook until onion is soft. Add salt, pepper, and next 4 ingredients.

2. Bring to a boil, cover with a tight lid, and place in oven.

3. Bake at 400° for 17 minutes. Discard sprigs and bay leaf. Use a fork to stir in remaining 1 tablespoon butter.

Yield: 4 servings

Spinach Casserole

2 (10-ounce) packages chopped spinach
1 (8-ounce) carton sour cream
½ cup freshly grated Parmesan cheese
2 teaspoons garlic salt
1 teaspoon dried basil
Buttered breadcrumbs for topping

1. Cook spinach according to package, omitting salt. Drain and press out water thoroughly. Place spinach in a greased casserole dish.

2. Mix in sour cream and next 3 ingredients. Top with breadcrumbs.

3. Bake at 350° for 30 minutes.

Yield: 4 to 6 servings

Zucchini Casserole

1. Cook zucchini in lightly salted boiling water for 10 minutes or until just tender. Drain. Remove ends and cut in half lengthwise. Arrange, cut side up, in a greased dish.

2. Mix together margarine and next 7 ingredients. Pour over zucchini. Spread breadcrumbs evenly over top. Dot with butter. Sprinkle with Parmesan cheese.

3. Bake at 350° for 45 minutes or until lightly browned and bubbly.

Yield: 8 to 10 servings

Good choices for herbs include chives, basil, tarragon, and oregano.

8 medium zucchini
4 tablespoons margarine, melted
½ cup tightly packed grated Cheddar cheese
½ cup tightly packed grated Swiss cheese
1 cup sour cream or plain yogurt
Pinch of salt
Pinch of paprika
½ cup chopped fresh herbs of choice
2 green onions, finely sliced including tops
1 cup breadcrumbs
Butter
Parmesan cheese for topping

Potpourri bags of net or lace can be lined with used laundry softener sheets before filling with herbs.

Autumn

Main Dishes

Amatriciana Pasta

1 yellow onion, finely chopped
2 tablespoons butter
3 tablespoons olive oil
2 ounces pancetta
2 (14.5-ounce) cans stewed tomatoes
½ tablespoon red bell pepper, chopped
1 pound pasta
2 tablespoons dried basil
3 tablespoons Parmesan cheese
3 tablespoons grated Romano cheese

1. Sauté onion in butter and oil. Add pancetta and sauté for 1 minute. Add tomatoes and bell pepper.

2. Cook pasta according to package. Drain.

3. Combine pasta with tomato mixture, basil, and cheeses. Toss. Serve immediately.

Yield: 4 servings

Baked Fish With Dill Sauce

1. Place fish in a greased baking dish. Spread butter evenly over fish. Top with parsley, onions, and dill.

2. Whip together flour and next 4 ingredients. Pour a third of sauce over fish.

3. Bake at 400° for 15 minutes. Add olive slices and dill seed to remaining sauce. Pour over fish and bake 10 to 12 minutes longer. Baste occasionally while baking.

Yield: 4 servings

Reduce fat by coating fish with nonstick cooking spray rather than spreading with butter.

4	pieces orange roughy
3	tablespoons butter, softened
⅓	cup chopped fresh parsley
2	green onions, chopped
1	teaspoon dried dill
1	tablespoon all-purpose flour
1	cup white wine
¼	cup heavy cream
½	teaspoon salt
⅛	teaspoon black pepper
½	cup sliced black olives
½	teaspoon dill seed

For an easy side dish for grilled fish, wash leeks to remove dirt and sand between the leaves. Slice into 1-inch chunks, and gently steam until tender. When leeks have cooled, add your favorite vinaigrette dressing.

Autumn

Sam's Venison Stew

4 pounds venison
2 cups all-purpose flour
3 tablespoons bacon fat
1½ cups hot water
1 cup red wine
1 large onion, chopped
1½ teaspoons salt
1 teaspoon lemon pepper
Pinch of dried thyme
Pinch of dried marjoram
Pinch of dried basil
3 carrots, quartered
3 potatoes, quartered
1 (7.3-ounce) jar sliced mushrooms, drained

1. Remove any bones or tendons from venison. Cut into bite-size pieces and roll in flour.

2. Brown meat in bacon fat in a cast iron pot. Add water and next 7 ingredients. Cover and bring to a boil. Reduce heat and simmer 2 hours.

3. Add carrot, potato, and mushrooms. Cover and simmer 60 minutes or until meat and vegetables are tender. Add extra hot water during cooking, if necessary.

4. Serve with hot cornsticks.

Yield: 6 servings

For a pasta topper, gather handfuls of your favorite herbs, discard tough stems, and place in blender. Add as much garlic as desired and a small amount of water. Toss with pasta or serve atop meat or vegetables.

Chicken Rosemary

1. Combine flour and next 4 ingredients in a large plastic storage bag. Add chicken and shake to coat.

2. Place chicken skin side down in a greased pan. Dot chicken with butter. Bake at 400° for 30 minutes.

3. While baking, boil water. Add bouillon and lemon juice. Remove chicken from oven and turn. Pour bouillon mixture over chicken. Sprinkle with rosemary. Bake 30 minutes longer.

Yield: 6 servings

1   cup all-purpose flour
1   tablespoon paprika
½   teaspoon dried oregano
1   teaspoon salt
½   teaspoon dried thyme
6   chicken breasts
Butter
⅓   cup water
1   chicken bouillon cube
Juice of ½ lemon
Dried rosemary

Store dried herbs whole. Crumble herbs by hand or in a mortar and pestle just before using them to release the natural oils.

Autumn

Italian-Stuffed Chicken Breasts

4 chicken breasts, boned and skinned
4 thin slices boiled ham
4 thin slices processed Swiss cheese
Crushed dried sage
1 medium tomato, peeled and chopped
⅓ cup Italian-style breadcrumbs
2 tablespoons Parmesan cheese
2 tablespoons minced fresh parsley
4 tablespoons margarine, melted

1. Flatten breasts to size of a slice of bread. Place a slice of ham and a slice of Swiss cheese on each breast. Top with a sprinkle of sage and some tomato.

2. Roll breasts to enclose filling. Skewer or tie closed. Combine breadcrumbs, Parmesan cheese, and parsley. Dip chicken in margarine and coat with breadcrumb mixture.

3. Place in a greased shallow baking pan. Bake at 350° for about 45 minutes.

Yield: 4 servings

Make Italian-style breadcrumbs by combining plain breadcrumbs with dried basil, oregano, savory, thyme, and marjoram.

Stuffed Cornish Game Hens

1. Wash hens. Rub each cavity with a small amount of salt.

2. To make stuffing, brown sausage and drain. Sauté onion, celery, and mushrooms in butter until tender. Mix in sausage.

3. Combine sausage mixture with salt and next 4 ingredients. Stuff hens.

4. Place hens in a Dutch oven. Pour in ½ inch of water. Steams hens for 25 to 30 minutes.

5. While steaming hens, prepare basting sauce by combining all ingredients. Transfer hens to an oven.

6. Bake at 350° until tender and evenly browned. Baste frequently with sauce while baking.

Yield: 6 servings

Hens

6 (22-ounce) Cornish game hens
Salt

Stuffing

½ pound pork sausage
½ cup chopped onion
½ cup chopped celery
1 cup sliced mushrooms
1½ sticks butter or margarine
½ teaspoon salt
½ teaspoon black pepper
Poultry seasoning to taste
1 (16-ounce) package bread stuffing
1 (14½-ounce) can chicken broth

Basting Sauce

½ cup chicken broth
½ cup finely chopped fresh parsley
4 tablespoons butter or margarine, melted

Autumn

Stuffed Bell Peppers

½ pound ground
   pork
8 large bell peppers
2 tablespoons butter
3 small onions,
   finely chopped
1 clove garlic, finely
   chopped
Salt and pepper to
   taste
2 tablespoons finely
   chopped fresh
   parsley
½ teaspoon dried
   oregano
2 tablespoons raisins
1½ tablespoons finely
   chopped pecans
1½ tablespoons finely
   chopped blanched
   almonds
1 cup sour cream
1 cup water, divided
⅔ cup finely
   chopped ham
3 cups breadcrumbs
2 eggs
Parmesan cheese for
   topping

1. Brown pork and drain.

2. Cut a thin slice from stem end of each bell pepper. Cut away core from thin slices. Finely chop remaining "meat" of thin slices and set aside. Remove seeds and pith from large section of peppers.

3. Cook pepper shells in boiling water for 4 to 5 minutes.

4. Melt butter in a skillet. Add onion, garlic, and finely chopped pepper. Cook until onion is transparent.

5. Add pork, salt, pepper, and next 6 ingredients. Stir in ½ cup water and bring to a boil. Reduce heat and simmer 10 minutes. Add ham and remaining ½ cup water. Simmer 5 minutes.

6. Remove from heat. Add breadcrumbs and eggs. Blend well. Stuff into pepper shells. Sprinkle with cheese.

7. Bake at 350° for 30 to 35 minutes or until thoroughly heated.

Yield: 8 servings

Eggplant Lasagna

1. Peel eggplants unless skin is tender. Cut into ½-inch-thick slices. Brush both sides of slices with 2½ tablespoons oil.

2. Place on a baking sheet and bake at 325° for 8 minutes. Brush remaining ½ tablespoon oil in a skillet. Add bell pepper, onion, and garlic and sauté.

3. Arrange half of eggplant slices in a 13x9x2-inch baking dish coated with non-stick cooking spray. Spread half of sautéed vegetables over slices. Add a layer of 4 noodles. Top with half of sauce. Sprinkle half of cheese on top. Repeat layers.

4. Bake at 350° for 45 minutes.

Yield: 12 servings

2 medium eggplants
3 tablespoons olive oil, divided
2 large bell peppers, sliced
2 onions, sliced
2 large cloves garlic, crushed
8 lasagna noodles, cooked al dente
1 (26-ounce) jar tomato and pesto sauce
⅓ cup Parmesan cheese

Pesto Pizza

1. Spread 1 tablespoon pesto and 2 tablespoons sauce over each tortilla. Evenly divide artichoke and remaining 5 ingredients over top of tortillas in order listed.

2. Place on baking sheets. Bake at 450° for 8 to 10 minutes or until edges browned and cheese melts.

Yield: 4 servings

¼ cup pesto, divided
½ cup spaghetti sauce, divided
4 flour tortillas
½ cup sliced artichoke hearts
½ cup diced turkey luncheon meat
1 medium tomato, seeded and diced
¼ cup chopped black olives
½ cup grated mozzarella cheese
¼ cup Parmesan cheese

Autumn

Harvest Vegetable Pie

2   bunches green
    onions, chopped
¼   cup extra virgin
    olive oil
3   small crookneck
    squash, sliced
2   small zucchini,
    sliced
6   large mushrooms,
    sliced
2   tomatoes, peeled,
    chopped, and
    drained
1   tablespoon
    chopped fresh
    basil
1   tablespoon
    chopped fresh
    parsley
Salt and pepper to
    taste
Seasonings to taste
1   (9-inch) pie shell,
    unbaked
1   cup mayonnaise
1   cup grated
    mozzarella cheese

1. Sauté onion in oil until tender. Remove onion. Sauté squash and zucchini.

2. Combine onion, squash, zucchini, mushrooms, and next 5 ingredients. Place mixture in pie shell.

3. Mix mayonnaise and cheese. Spread over top of vegetables. Bake for 60 minutes at 350°.

Yield: 8 servings

When packing clothes away for the
season, put small bags of dried herbs in the boxes—
especially in handbags and luggage.

Autumn

Spinach and Eggs Grisanti

1. Cook spinach according to package. Drain well, pressing out as much liquid as possible.

2. Cook bacon until crisp. Drain on absorbent paper.

3. Heat oil in a skillet. Add garlic and sauté until garlic is golden brown. Mix in spinach, black pepper, salt, and monosodium glutamate.

4. Spread mixture over bottom of skillet and sprinkle 1 tablespoon cheese over top. Cook, turning spinach over, until very hot.

5. Add eggs and continue turning mixture until eggs cook thoroughly. Crumble bacon and stir into mixture. Drain excess oil from skillet.

6. Turn spinach onto a warm serving platter and sprinkle with remaining 2 tablespoons cheese.

Yield: 2 to 3 servings

The more liquid you press from the spinach, the better the results from this easy dish.

1 (10-ounce) package frozen chopped spinach
2 slices bacon
3 tablespoons olive oil
1 small clove garlic, minced
1/8 teaspoon black pepper
1/4 teaspoon salt
1/4 teaspoon monosodium glutamate
3 tablespoons freshly grated Parmesan cheese, divided
2 eggs

Autumn

Amaretto Mint Pound Cake

7 ounces amaretto, divided
1 (18-ounce) package yellow cake mix with pudding
¼ cup vegetable oil
5 tablespoons finely chopped fresh chocolate mint
4 eggs
1 cup powdered sugar
4 tablespoons butter, melted
Sprigs of fresh chocolate mint for garnish

1. Blend 6 ounces amaretto and next 3 ingredients with an electric mixer at medium speed for 3 minutes. Beat in eggs one at a time and blend until smooth.

2. Pour mixture into a greased and floured Bundt pan. Bake at 325° for 60 minutes.

3. To make glaze, mix sugar, butter, and remaining 1 ounce amaretto until smooth. Drizzle glaze over warm cake. Garnish.

Yield: 8 to 10 servings

Brown Autumn Bars

1. Combine flour, butter, and ¼ cup brown sugar. Pack mixture into a well-greased 13x9x2-inch pan to form a crust. Bake at 350° for 10 minutes.

2. Beat eggs until frothy. Mix in remaining 2 cups brown sugar, coconut, and next 5 ingredients. Stir in lemon juice and zest. Spread over slightly cooled crust.

3. Bake at 350° for 25 minutes. Cool before cutting.

Yield: 8 to 10 servings

2	cups all-purpose flour
1	stick butter
2¼	cups packed brown sugar, divided
3	eggs
1	cup grated coconut
½	teaspoon salt
2	tablespoons sesame seed
1	tablespoon caraway seed
1	cup raisins
½	cup chopped walnuts
2	tablespoons lemon juice
1	teaspoon lemon zest

Lemon/Orange Baskets

Cut the top out of the fruit so as to form a handle for the basket. Scoop out the insides. Let dry about 1 week. Fill with bags of mulling spices or lemon drops.

Autumn

Fresh Apple Cake With Rose Geranium

Cake

2   cups sugar
2   sticks butter,
    softened
2   eggs
2   cups all-purpose
    flour
1   teaspoon
    cinnamon
1   tablespoon baking
    soda
4   cups chopped,
    unpeeled tart
    apples
2   dried rose
    geranium leaves,
    crumbled, or 6
    fresh, chopped

Icing

1   stick butter
1   cup packed brown
    sugar
¾   cup chopped nuts
¼   cup all-purpose
    flour
¼   cup water
3   fresh rose
    geranium leaves,
    chopped
Red bud blossoms or
    other edible
    flowers for garnish

1. Cream sugar and butter. Beat in eggs. Mix in flour, cinnamon, and baking soda. Stir in apples and rose geranium.

2. Pour into a greased and floured 13x9x2-inch pan.

3. Bake at 350° for 40 to 50 minutes or until a toothpick inserted near the center comes out clean.

4. To prepare icing, combine butter and next 5 ingredients in a saucepan. Cook about 10 minutes.

5. Pour over hot cake and bake 3 minutes more. Top each serving with a dollop of whipped cream and garnish.

Yield: 15 to 18 servings

Use this recipe to expand the pleasures of the apple harvest with the delicate addition of rose geranium leaves. The last touch of red bud blossoms will leave your guests feeling pampered.

Josie's Moist Cake

1. Sift together flour and next 4 ingredients. Stir in wheat germ.

2. In a separate bowl, combine apple and next 5 ingredients. Mix in walnuts. Moisten bran cereal with hot water. Combine bran cereal with molasses and add to apple mixture. Stir in dry ingredients with a wooden spoon. Mix well.

3. Place in a greased 13x9x2-inch pan. Bake at 350° for 50 minutes or until cake pulls away from sides of pan. Cool on a rack. Sprinkle with powdered sugar.

Yield: 8 to 10 servings

Other fruits can replace up to half of the apples. Sunflower seeds or other nuts can replace the walnuts.

2   cups whole wheat flour
2   teaspoons baking soda
1   teaspoon cinnamon
½   teaspoon nutmeg
1   teaspoon salt
¼   cup wheat germ (optional)
4   large cooking apples, diced
1   cup packed brown sugar
½   cup sugar
½   cup oil
2   eggs, beaten
1   teaspoon vanilla
1   cup chopped walnuts
¼   cup bran cereal
1   tablespoon molasses
    Powdered sugar for topping (optional)

Mystery Fudge Cake

1½ sticks margarine, softened
2 cups sugar
3 eggs
3 tablespoons chopped fresh mint
1 teaspoon mint extract
2 cups coarsely grated green tomatoes
1 teaspoon vanilla
½ cup milk
2½ cups all-purpose flour
½ cup cocoa
2½ teaspoons baking powder
½ teaspoon baking soda
1 teaspoon salt
1 teaspoon cinnamon
1 cup chopped walnuts

1. Cream margarine and sugar. Beat in eggs one at a time. Mix in fresh mint and next 4 ingredients.

2. In a separate bowl, combine flour and remaining 6 ingredients. Stir dry ingredients into batter. Pour into a greased and floured 10-inch tube pan.

3. Bake at 350° for 50 to 60 minutes or until a toothpick inserted in the center comes out clean.

Yield: 12 servings

Let them rave about the taste before you reveal the mystery.

Chocolate mint is a delicious addition to coffee.

Naomi's Cooked Custard With Lemon Verbena

1. Combine sugar and cornstarch. Stir in ¼ cup milk.

2. Beat eggs slightly in a separate bowl. Add remaining 3¾ cups milk to eggs. Slowly beat sugar mixture into egg mixture with a wire whip.

3. Cook over medium-low heat, stirring constantly, until mixture thickens and coats a wooden spoon. Add vanilla and lemon verbena. Cool before serving.

Yield: 8 servings

¾ cup sugar
1 tablespoon cornstarch
4 cups milk, divided
3 eggs
½ teaspoon vanilla
2 teaspoons finely chopped lemon verbena

Quick Apple Tart

1. Roll out pastry on a baking sheet. Sprinkle with rosemary.

2. Attractively arrange apple slices, leaving a ½-inch border. Spread preserves over slices. Sprinkle with cinnamon. Fold pastry border over apples.

4. Bake at 400° for 15 minutes or until pastry has puffed and is golden brown. Serve warm with whipped cream or ice cream.

Yield: 4 to 6 servings

1 (8½-ounce) frozen puff pastry sheet
3 tablespoons chopped fresh rosemary
6 Rome apples, sliced
¼ cup apricot preserves
Cinnamon to taste

Autumn

Pumpkin Bars

Bars

2 cups sugar
½ cup vegetable oil
1 (16-ounce) can pumpkin
4 eggs, beaten
2 cups biscuit baking mix
2 teaspoons cinnamon
½ cup raisins

Cream Cheese Frosting

1 (3-ounce) package cream cheese
5 tablespoons margarine, softened
1 tablespoon milk
1 teaspoon vanilla
2 cups powdered sugar

1. Beat together sugar and next 3 ingredients with an electric mixer on medium speed for 1 minute, scraping sides occasionally.

2. Stir in biscuit baking mix, cinnamon, and raisins. Pour into a greased 15½x10½x1-inch jellyroll pan.

3. Bake at 350° for 25 to 30 minutes or until a toothpick inserted in the center comes out clean. Cool.

4. To make frosting, mix cream cheese and next 3 ingredients until creamy. Stir in powdered sugar. Frost bars before cutting into squares. Refrigerate.

Yield: 50 servings

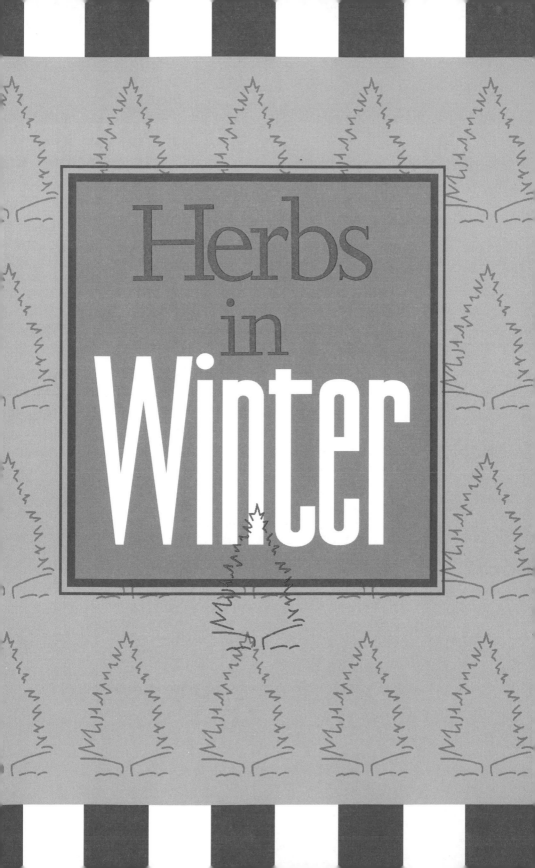

Herbs in Winter

n most of North America, winter offers us a contrast from the other months: cooler, darker and wetter with either snow or rain. Dried herbs keep well as do the favored seasonal vegetables, potatoes, and other roots. Long slow cooking times for soups, stews, and braised meats makes the most of all ingredients' flavors.

🌲 Gather with friends or family around the table on a long winter night and the ordinary becomes festive thanks to laughter, light, and good food.

🌲 On a cold winter's night, toss dried lavender flowers, leaves, and stems in the roaring fire.

🌲 Tuck dried herb sprigs into ribbons on packages for holiday gifts. Traditionally, rosemary was a popular herb at Christmas: stirred into Christmas puddings, used to flavor wine and ale, and hung in boughs as Christmas decorations. Tuck it into cards for remembrance.

🌲 Satisfy that urge to watch things grow by starting a small pot of herbs from seed in a sunny window or under fluorescent lights. Later, remove them to the balcony or garden or make a gift to someone special.

The Herbs of Christmas

In the time Christ was born, herbs were important in daily life. Through the centuries, legends have remained about herbs and the celebration of Christmas.

Christmas Eve Happiness: Legend recommends having rosemary in your home on Christmas Eve to bring happiness to the family.

A Manger for the Christ Child: Joseph prepared the manger for the Christ child by lining the makeshift bed with bedstraw, wild grasses, and fragrant herbs that were natural insect repellents. Among them, pennyroyal is said to have bloomed on Christmas Day. Wild thyme symbolizes the bravery of the Christ child and his parents. The grasses included horehound, chamomile, and sweet woodruff. Chamomile represents patience. Vanilla-scented sweet woodruff symbolizes humility.

Santa Lucia and Rue: The Swedes begin their Christmas season on December 13, the day of Santa Lucia with whom the herb rue is associated. Rue represents vision, virginity, and repentance.

Lavender's Smell: Lavender's refreshing scent is said to have sprung from the day when Mary first washed her baby's clothes, spreading them on lavender bushes to dry.

Gifts of the Wise Men: They came bearing precious gifts of frankincense and myrrh. These were prized treasures — each a gummy tree resin — in ancient trade. Frankincense was used to perfume the air for religious rites and as medicine in Asia. The Egyptians and Hebrews found uses for the rare myrrh in incense, cosmetics, perfume, medicine, and for embalming the dead.

Winter

Chili Dip

1 (15-ounce) can
chili without
beans
2 (3-ounce)
packages cream
cheese
½ cup green chile
salsa or jalapeño
pepper salsa
1 (2¼-ounce) can
sliced black olives,
drained
Chopped fresh
cilantro

1. Combine chili and next 3 ingredients. Heat and stir.

2. Sprinkle with cilantro. Serve with corn chips.

Yield: *about 3 cups*

Keep dip warm by serving in a mini crock pot.

Cheese Spread

2 strips bacon
1 cup grated
American cheese
¼ cup slivered
almonds, toasted
2 green onions
including stems,
chopped
½ cup mayonnaise
¼ cup chopped fresh
parsley

1. Cook bacon until crisp. Drain and crumble. Combine bacon and remaining 5 ingredients.

2. Spread on crackers or French bread. Broil until bubbly.

Yield: *4 to 6 servings*

Cheese Twists

1. Roll biscuits into 10-inch strips. Twist 2 strips together and seal ends. Brush with egg. Sprinkle cheese and caraway seed over top.

2. Place on a baking sheet. Bake at 375° until golden. Serve warm.

Yield: 5 or 6 twists

1 (10- or 12-ounce) can refrigerated biscuits
1 egg, lightly beaten
½ cup grated Cheddar cheese
1 teaspoon caraway, poppy, or sesame seed

Herbed Cheese

1. Combine garlic and next 4 ingredients in a food processor. Process until finely chopped.

2. Add cream cheese and milk. Blend until smooth.

3. Refrigerate in a small covered dish at least 24 hours. Stores in the refrigerator up to 1 week. Serve with crackers.

Yield: 4 to 6 servings

If a food processor is not available, chop vegetables and herbs with a knife. Blend into milk and cheese.

1 small clove garlic
1 green onion, quartered
¼ cup fresh basil
¼ cup fresh parsley
1 tablespoon fresh oregano, or ½ teaspoon dried
1 (8-ounce) package cream cheese
1 tablespoon milk

For birthday bashes, crush coriander seed—symbol of immortality—in bottom of serving cups for hot coffee or espresso.

Herb Cheesecake

3 (8-ounce) packages cream cheese, softened
2 cups sour cream, divided
1 (10¾-ounce) can condensed cream of celery soup
3 eggs
½ cup Romano cheese
2 cloves garlic, minced
1 tablespoon cornstarch
2 tablespoons finely chopped fresh basil, or 2 teaspoons crushed dried
1 tablespoon finely chopped fresh thyme, or 1 teaspoon crushed dried
1 teaspoon finely chopped fresh tarragon, or ¼ teaspoon crushed dried
½ teaspoon cracked black pepper
Red bell pepper slices, lemon twists, or fresh herbs for garnish

1. Combine cream cheese, 1 cup sour cream, and soup in a food processor or a large mixing bowl. Blend at medium speed until smooth.

2. Add eggs and next 7 ingredients. Blend until smooth.

3. Pour into a greased 9-inch springform pan. Place on a jellyroll pan. Bake at 350° for 60 minutes or until lightly browned.

4. Turn off oven and let stand in oven 30 minutes. Remove from oven and cool in pan on a rack.

5. Cover and refrigerate at least 4 hours or overnight. When ready to serve, remove from pan. Spread remaining 1 cup sour cream over the top. Garnish.

6. Serve with crackers, Melba toast, or fresh vegetables.

Yield: 10 to 12 servings

This cheesecake is wonderful for a party.

A recipe that redefines cheesecake for the appetizer table

Herb Spread

1. Combine all ingredients. Refrigerate overnight to allow flavors to blend. Taste and adjust seasoning as needed.

2. Serve at room temperature with crackers.

Yield: 4 to 6 servings

Sweet marjoram, rosemary, salad burnet, dill, thyme, and tarragon are a few good choices of herbs to use in this recipe.

1   cup chopped fresh parsley
3   tablespoons chopped fresh chives
1   (8-ounce) package light or fat free cream cheese, softened
3   tablespoons light mayonnaise
Dash of hot pepper sauce
2   tablespoons lemon juice
Sprigs of fresh herbs of choice

Philly Pâté

1. Mix cream cheese and meat until well blended. Add olives and remaining 4 ingredients. Mix well.

2. Place in a greased 3-cup ring mold and chill.

3. Unmold. Serve with crackers.

Yield: 4 to 6 servings

During the Christmas holiday, decorate with fresh parsley and pimiento to resemble a wreath.

1   (8-ounce) package cream cheese
1   (12-ounce) can spiced luncheon meat, ground
½   cup chopped stuffed Spanish olives
2   tablespoons finely chopped onion
2   teaspoons Worcestershire sauce
2   teaspoons lemon juice
¼   teaspoon powdered thyme

Winter

Marinated Christmas Tree

2 bunches broccoli
2 heads cauliflower
1 cup cider vinegar
1 tablespoon sugar
1 tablespoon dried dill
1 tablespoon salt
1 teaspoon coarsely ground black pepper
1 clove garlic, minced
1½ cups vegetable oil
Cherry tomatoes for garnish

1. Separate broccoli and cauliflower into small flowerets. Reserve 1 broccoli stalk.

2. Combine vinegar and next 6 ingredients. Pour mixture over broccoli and cauliflower.

3. Cover and refrigerate 24 hours, basting vegetables with marinade occasionally. Drain.

4. Arrange broccoli on a tray in the shape of a Christmas tree. Use broccoli stalk for a tree trunk. Arrange cauliflower around tree as a background. Decorate tree with tomatoes as ornaments. Chill.

Yield: 10 to 12 servings

Serve this dish at a brunch, buffet, or cocktail party. It's a simple vegetable tray, but no one will know but you.

Cinnamon-Applesauce Ornaments

Mix 1 cup cinnamon and 1 (8-ounce) can of applesauce together until dough is formed. Add glue to make it stay together. Roll out and cut with cookie cutters. Poke holes in top for hanging. Let air dry completely for at least one week. Decorate with paint, if desired.

Spiced Pecans

1. Place butter in a 2-quart micro-wave-safe dish. Microwave on high power for 1 to 2 minutes or until melted.

2. Mix in salt and next 6 ingredients. Add pecans and stir well to coat.

3. Microwave, uncovered, on high power for 6 to 8 minutes or until thoroughly heated. Stir once halfway through cooking time.

4. Cool. Store in tightly sealed jars for up to 1 month at room temperature.

Yield: 2 cups

1   stick unsalted butter
½   teaspoon salt
2   tablespoons Worcestershire sauce
1   teaspoon hot pepper sauce
½   teaspoon cinnamon
Dash of ground cloves
Dash of garlic powder
1   tablespoon chopped fresh rosemary, or 1 teaspoon dried
2   cups whole, shelled pecans

Spinach Dip

1. Combine all ingredients in a bowl. Cover and refrigerate overnight to allow flavors to blend.

2. Serve with tortilla chips.

Yield: 6 to 8 servings

1   (10-ounce) package frozen spinach, thawed and squeezed dry
1   clove garlic, pressed
½   cup regular, low-fat, or fat-free mayonnaise
½   teaspoon cayenne pepper

Winter

Cranberry Meat Balls

2 pounds ground
beef
½ cup breadcrumbs
2 eggs
½ cup water
2 tablespoons
chopped fresh
parsley
Pinch of ground sage
1 large onion, diced
1 (16-ounce) bottle
chili sauce
1 (16-ounce) can
jellied cranberry
sauce

1. Combine beef and next 5 ingredients. Form into small balls and place on a baking sheet. Bake at 350° for 20 minutes.

2. Sauté onion in a Dutch oven. Add meat balls, chili sauce, and cranberry sauce. Simmer about 4 hours.

Yield: 18 to 20 servings

Tarragon Swedish Meatballs

1 (3-pound)
package frozen
cooked meatballs,
thawed
3 (10¾-ounce) cans
condensed cream
of mushroom
soup
1 pound
mushrooms, sliced
1¼ cups sour cream
Salt and pepper to
taste
Pinch of cayenne
pepper
¼ cup chopped fresh
tarragon
1½ cups vermouth

1. Combine all ingredients in a Dutch oven. Bring to a boil. Reduce heat and simmer 30 minutes.

2. Serve warm in a chafing dish.

Yield: about 8 dozen meatballs

Herbed Honey

1. Wrap lemon balm and next 5 ingredients in a cheesecloth bag. Add bag to honey in a saucepan. Cook over low heat about 30 minutes, stirring occasionally.

2. Transfer bag to a 1-quart container. Slowly pour in honey. Cover and let stand at room temperature for 1 week.

3. Remove and discard bag. Pour honey into 1-cup containers and seal.

Yield: *about 4 cups*

A jar of herbed honey makes a nice Christmas gift.

4 sprigs fresh lemon balm or lemon verbena
2 cloves garlic, quartered
1 dried bay leaf
1½ teaspoons crushed dried basil
1 teaspoon cloves
Zest of 1 lemon
4 cups honey

Mustard Dill Sauce

1. Blend mustards and sugar in a blender or food processor.

2. Continue to process and slowly add oil. Add vinegar slowly. Mix in dill, salt, and pepper. Adjust flavor, as desired, by adding more sugar, vinegar, or salt and pepper.

3. Serve with herring, smoked salmon, or lox.

Yield: *about 1 cup*

⅓ cup hot Dijon mustard
⅓ cup sweet German or Swedish mustard
1 tablespoon sugar
3 tablespoons olive oil
2 tablespoons white wine vinegar
2 tablespoons minced fresh dill
Salt and pepper to taste

Winter

Herb Fingers

24 slices white or wheat bread, crusts removed
1 stick butter or margarine
2 tablespoons Parmesan cheese
1¼ teaspoons dried oregano
1¼ teaspoons dried basil
½ teaspoon onion or garlic powder
¼ teaspoon dried chives

1. Cut each slice of bread into 3 strips; set aside.

2. In a small pan, combine butter and remaining 5 ingredients over low heat. When melted, brush on bread strips.

3. Place on a baking sheet. Bake at 325° for 15 minutes or until golden. Cool. Store in an airtight container.

Yield: 72 fingers

Variation: Cube bread to make croutons. Use extra amounts of sauce ingredients, if needed.

Lemon Pepper Cocktail Breadsticks

1 tablespoon lemon pepper
¼ cup Dijon mustard
3 tablespoons butter, melted
1 (11-ounce) can refrigerated breadstick dough

1. Combine lemon pepper, mustard, and butter; set aside.

2. Unroll dough. Cut dough crosswise and then cut each stick lengthwise. Separate strips. Twist each strip slightly and place on a baking sheet. Generously brush with mustard mixture.

3. Bake at 350° for 15 minutes or until lightly browned.

Yield: 32 breadsticks

Lemon Poppy Seed Muffins

1. Combine flour and next 3 ingredients.

2. In a separate bowl, mix together milk and next 6 ingredients. Add to dry ingredients. Blend to just moisten.

3. Spoon into a greased muffin pan. Bake at 400° for 20 to 25 minutes.

4. Remove from pan and dust with powdered sugar.

Yield: 12 muffins

1¾ cup all-purpose flour
⅔ cup granulated sugar
2 tablespoons poppy seed
2 teaspoons baking powder
1 cup milk
¼ cup oil
¼ teaspoon salt
1 tablespoon lemon zest
2 tablespoons lemon juice
2 teaspoons chopped lemon balm
1 egg, beaten
Powdered sugar for topping

Dried Fruit Peel Cutouts

Pull off large pieces of peel from fruit, such as oranges, limes, lemons, or grapefruit. Cut out with miniature cookie cutters. Let air dry or dry in the dehydrator. Use for holiday decorations.

Winter

Ray's Healthy Muffins

1 cup whole wheat pastry flour
1 teaspoon baking soda
¼ teaspoon baking powder
2 teaspoons cinnamon
2 tablespoons wheat germ
2 tablespoons bran
¼ cup applesauce
¼ cup fructose
¼ cup egg substitute
⅔ cup fat-free buttermilk
1 teaspoon vanilla
1 cup mashed banana
½ cup diced apple
½ cup raisins

1. Sift together flour and next 3 ingredients. Stir in wheat germ and bran.

2. In a separate bowl, beat applesauce and next 4 ingredients until well blended. Stir mixture into dry ingredients until just blended. Fold in banana, apple, and raisins.

3. Spoon batter into paper-lined muffin cups, filling them about two-thirds full. Bake at 325° for 25 to 30 minutes or until a tooth-pick inserted in the center of a muffin comes out clean.

Yield: 16 muffins

Traditionally, oregano was prescribed for stomach and headaches. In the Middle Ages, oregano was strewn on the floor when someone was ill because it was believed to have antiseptic qualities.

French Spice Bread

1. Boil water. Add to anise seed and soak for 5 minutes.

2. Combine apricot and honey and add to warm anise seed mixture.

3. Sift together whole wheat flour and remaining 5 ingredients. Add dry ingredients to anise mixture. Stir until smooth.

4. Pour batter into a greased 9x5-inch loaf pan or 2 greased small loaf pans. Bake at 350° for 40 to 50 minutes or until a toothpick inserted near center of loaf comes out clean.

5. Remove from pan and cool completely on a rack. Wrap tightly in plastic wrap. Let stand at least 24 hours before slicing. Slice very thin.

Yield: *1 large loaf or 2 small loaves*

Enclose wrapped bread in a zip-top plastic bag and it will store well for a long time.

¾	cup water
1	teaspoon anise seed
1½	cups chopped dried apricots
1¼	cups honey
1½	cups whole wheat flour
1	cup all-purpose flour
2	teaspoons baking soda
1	teaspoon cinnamon
1	teaspoon nutmeg
¼	teaspoon ground cloves

Colonial Americans used peppermint as medicine, and mint tea was substituted when the Chinese variety was taxed by the British government.

Herbed Pecan Red Onion Bread

1	(¼-ounce) package active dry yeast
3	cups bread flour
1½	teaspoons sugar
1½	teaspoons salt
1	cup plus 1 tablespoon milk
½	cup chopped red onion
¾	cup chopped pecans
¼	cup chopped fresh Italian parsley
¼	cup finely chopped fresh rosemary

1. Combine yeast and next 3 ingredients. Heat milk until warm. Add milk and remaining 4 ingredients to dry ingredients. Mix well. Knead until smooth.

2. Place in a greased bowl and cover. Let rise until doubled in size. Punch down dough. Form into 1 large or 2 small loaves.

3. Place in greased loaf pans or on a greased baking sheet. Let rise 30 minutes or until almost doubled.

4. Bake at 350° for about 20 minutes. Lower heat to 325° and bake 10 to 15 minutes or until browned. Remove from pans and cool on a rack.

Yield: 1 large or 2 small loaves

Over the centuries, garlic has been food, medium of exchange, medicine, and object of worship. The Roman legions ate garlic to make them tough. In the Middle Ages, garlic was a remedy against vampires and the plague. Garlic was applied as an antiseptic during World War I and proved a lifesaver. Recent studies have confirmed garlic's power as a natural antibiotic. The health benefits outweigh the problems of garlic breath so make friends with others who love the herb.

Savory Brunch Pull-apart

1. Combine cheese, sesame seed, and basil. Add about one-third of mixture to a well-greased 10-inch tube pan. Turn pan to coat bottom and sides.

2. Place 10 rolls in pan. Drizzle with 2 tablespoons of margarine. Sprinkle with half of remaining cheese mixture. Sprinkle with bacon bits. Add remaining rolls. Drizzle with remaining 2 tablespoons margarine. Sprinkle remaining cheese mixture over top. Cover.

3. Let dough thaw and rise 12 to 24 hours in refrigerator. Before baking, uncover and let stand at room temperature 30 minutes.

4. Bake at 350° for 20 minutes. Cover with foil and bake 10 to 15 minutes or until golden. Remove from pan. Cool slightly on rack. Serve warm.

Yield: 10 to 12 servings

¼ cup Parmesan cheese
3 tablespoons sesame seed
½ teaspoon crushed dried basil
1 (30-ounce) package frozen unbaked rolls, divided
4 tablespoons margarine, melted, divided
2 tablespoons bacon bits (optional)

Cinnamon Heart Wreaths for Valentine's Day

Cut out a large heart from white card stock. Glue cinnamon sticks on it to fit the shape. Add cloves along the border and flowers with a bow on top. Use as a centerpiece or door hanging.

Monkey Bread

3 (10- or 12-ounce) cans refrigerated biscuits
Sugar to taste
Cinnamon to taste
Chopped nuts to taste, divided
1 stick butter
½ cup liquid brown sugar

1. Separate biscuits and cut each in fourths using a scissors. Combine sugar and cinnamon. Roll biscuit pieces in cinnamon mixture. Place a layer of pieces in a greased tube pan.

2. Sprinkle with some of nuts. Place remaining pieces in pan. Sprinkle with remaining nuts. Heat butter and brown sugar to a boil. Pour over biscuits.

3. Bake at 350° for 30 minutes.

Yield: 10 to 12 servings

Lemon/Pineapple Punch

1 (6-ounce) package lemon-flavored jello
4 cups hot water, divided
2 cups sugar
2 quarts pineapple juice
2 cups lemon juice
1 ounce almond extract
3 quarts ginger ale
Sprigs of fresh mint or lemon balm

1. Dissolve jello in 2 cups hot water. Dissolve sugar in remaining 2 cups hot water.

2. Combine jello and sugar mixtures with pineapple juice, lemon juice, and almond extract. Mix well and freeze.

3. Remove from freezer 2 to 3 hours before serving. Mix in ginger ale and mint sprigs when ready to serve. Punch will be slushy. Do not add ice cubes.

Yield: 48 (four-ounce) servings

Hot Spiced Lavender Tea

1. To prepare infusion, cover lavender buds with water in a saucepan. Cover and heat. Simmer 15 to 20 minutes. Strain.

2. To make concentrate, heat and stir tea and next 3 ingredients until dissolved. Add lemon juice and infusion. Refrigerate until serving time.

3. Complete tea by combining concentrate and remaining 4 ingredients. Heat and simmer 30 minutes.

Yield: about 75 (six-ounce) servings

Use leftover lavender buds in a simmering potpourri.

Lavender Infusion

1   cup fresh lavender buds
3   cups water

Concentrate

2   quarts strong prepared tea
1⅓ cups powdered orange-flavored breakfast drink
1   teaspoon powdered cloves
1   (9-ounce) package red hot candies
Juice of 1 large lemon
3   cups lavender infusion

Tea

Concentrate
2   gallons apple cider
½   gallon low-calorie cranberry juice cocktail
½   gallon water
Sugar substitute to taste

The Virgin Mary placed her blue cloak to dry on a rosemary bush and from that day, it is said the plant's flowers were blue instead of white.

Orange/Clove Tea Mix

¼   cup loose black tea
2   tablespoons whole
     cloves
Dried zest of 1 orange

 1. Combine all ingredients.

2. Store in a tightly covered container until ready to use.

Dry zest thoroughly before using. Tea will keep for several months and makes a nice gift.

Variations: Lemon/Mint Tea: ¼ cup loose black tea, 4 tablespoons dried mint, and dried zest of 1 lemon.

Lemon/Allspice Tea: ¼ cup loose black tea, 1 tablespoon whole allspice, and dried zest of 1 lemon.

Anise/Cinnamon Tea: ¼ cup loose black tea, 1 tablespoon anise seed, and a 4-inch cinnamon stick.

For an all-purpose seasoning, keep a bottle of burnt sugar on hand to season soups, gravies, and sauces. Drop a few cloves, a bay leaf, thyme, and sage into the bottle while the syrup is hot and you will always have seasoning at a minute's notice. (To burn sugar, put 1 cup of sugar in an iron skillet, and place on stove. Let it melt and turn deep brown. Add 1/2 cup water, and cook a few minutes longer. Stir carefully because it may bubble up. Remove from heat, and cool.)

Soups, Sandwiches, Salads

Basil Bean Soup

1. In a large saucepan, sauté onion and carrot in 1 tablespoon oil until onion starts to brown. Add potato and next 5 ingredients. Cover and cook over low heat for about 60 minutes.

2. In a separate bowl, combine tomato paste and next 3 ingredients. Slowly beat in remaining 2 tablespoons oil. Continue beating while slowly adding about 2 cups of hot soup.

3. Pour mixture into saucepan and mix. Add beans. Simmer 15 minutes. Serve with crusty French bread.

Yield: 6 to 8 servings

2   cups chopped onion
2   cups chopped carrot
3   tablespoons olive oil, divided
1   cup chopped potato
2   quarts water
2   cups fresh or frozen cut green beans
1   cup uncooked macaroni
½   teaspoon salt
¼   teaspoon dried thyme
¼   cup tomato paste
4   cloves garlic, minced
3   tablespoons chopped fresh basil
¼   cup Parmesan cheese
1   (16-ounce) can white beans, drained

Winter

Green Split Pea Soup

2 quarts water
4 teaspoons or cubes chicken bouillon
2 cloves garlic, minced
4 small carrots, sliced
4 medium potatoes, peeled and diced
1 cup chopped onion
2 teaspoons dried oregano
1 teaspoon dried rosemary
2 teaspoons dried parsley
2 (16-ounce) packages green split peas
Salt to taste

1. Combine water and next 8 ingredients in a large pot. Bring to a boil. Reduce to low heat and cook uncovered about 45 minutes.

2. Add peas. Continue cooking 45 minutes. Salt to taste.

Yield: 6 to 8 servings

This soup is good in the winter. It stores well in the freezer.

Rosemary Mushroom Soup

 1. Sauté mushrooms in butter. Add garlic and rosemary.

2. Mix in soup and cream. Heat slowly, stirring constantly. Add paprika. Heat until very hot.

3. Remove from heat and sprinkle with chives. Garnish each serving.

Yield: 4 to 6 servings

1 cup sliced fresh mushrooms
1 stick butter or margarine
2 cloves garlic
1 tablespoon chopped fresh rosemary
1 (10¾-ounce) can condensed cream of mushroom soup
1 cup light cream
½ teaspoon hot paprika
¼ cup chopped fresh chives
Sprigs of fresh parsley and rosemary for garnish

Pomegranate/Bayleaf Garland

Materials needed: 2 feet floral wire, 8 to 10 dried, small pomegranates, 50 to 60 bay leaves, 12 to 15 nutmegs, 20 dried apple slices, 2 yards raffia for bows. Optional: cinnamon/applesauce gingerbread people.

1. Using a tiny drill bit, drill small holes through pomegranates from side to side. Repeat for nutmegs.

2. Thread wire through a big-eyed needle.

3. String dried materials as follows, beginning and ending with a pomegranate: (1 pomegranate, 10 to 12 bay leaves, 1 cinnamon person, 2 apple slices, 3 nutmegs, 10 to 12 bay leaves, pomegranate)

4. Repeat until wire is full, leaving enough free to make a loop of wire at each end.

5. Tie a raffia bow onto each end by securing to wire loop.

Hint: Before stringing, wind wire on one end around a wooden match to hold items until stringing is complete.

Winter

White Bean Soup

1 pound dried white navy beans
2 tablespoons butter
¼ cup olive oil
1½ cups chopped leeks
3 large cloves garlic, finely chopped
1 cup chopped carrot
1 cup chopped celery
3 smoked ham hocks, excess fat removed
4 cups beef broth
2 cups chicken broth
2 cups water
½ teaspoon chopped fresh sage, or ¼ teaspoon dried
½ teaspoon chopped fresh basil, or ¼ teaspoon dried
½ teaspoon chopped fresh marjoram, or ¼ teaspoon dried
½ teaspoon chopped fresh winter savory, or ¼ teaspoon dried
1 dried bay leaf

1. Cover beans with cold water and soak overnight.

2. Drain beans. Heat butter and oil in a large saucepan or Dutch oven over medium-low heat. Add leeks and cook 1 minute. Add garlic, carrot, and celery and cook 5 minutes. Mix in beans, ham hocks, and remaining 8 ingredients. Bring to a boil. Reduce heat and cover. Simmer 1 hour, 30 minutes or until beans are tender.

3. Cool mixture. Discard bay leaf. Remove ham hocks. Cut meat from hocks and chop. Set aside. Puree 4 cups of soup in a food processor. Return puree to soup. Add ham pieces. Reheat to serve.

Yield: 6 to 8 servings

Herbed Party Sandwiches

1. Combine cream cheese and next 3 ingredients. Spread over bread slices.

2. Slice bread lengthwise into 3 pieces. Sprinkle with paprika. Garnish.

Yield: 12 to 14 servings

Freezing bread slightly makes cutting off crusts easier.

1 (8-ounce) package cream cheese, softened
1 tablespoon prepared horseradish
Freshly ground black pepper
Fresh salad burnet leaves
Sliced whole wheat bread, crusts removed
Paprika
Sprigs of salad burnet for garnish

Parsley And Bacon Sandwiches

1. Cook bacon until crisp. Drain and crumble. Mix bacon with parsley, garlic powder, Worcestershire sauce, and enough mayonnaise to achieve a spreading consistency.

2. Spread one side of each slice of bread with butter. Divide parsley mixture evenly over butter on half the bread slices. Top with remaining slices.

3. Cover with a damp cloth and refrigerate for 24 hours, or wrap and freeze. Cut into halves or quarters.

Yield: 8 to 10 sandwiches

1 pound bacon
2 bunches parsley, finely chopped
1 teaspoon garlic powder, or 1 large clove garlic, pressed
1 tablespoon Worcestershire sauce
Mayonnaise
1 loaf sliced fresh bread, crusts removed
Butter

Winter

Verlie's Cranberry Salad

4   oranges
1   pound fresh
    cranberries
2½ cups sugar
3   (3-ounce)
    packages cherry-
    flavored jello
1   (¼-ounce)
    envelope
    unflavored gelatin
2   cups chopped
    pecans
2   (8-ounce) cans
    crushed pineapple,
    drained
Fresh herb greens:
    parsley, salad
    burnet, and lemon
    thyme

1. Peel 3 oranges, leaving skin of 1 orange intact. Grind oranges and cranberries in a blender. Drain. Mix in sugar and let stand 2 hours.

2. Prepare jello according to package, using water or fruit juices. Stir in unflavored gelatin until dissolved. Add cranberry, orange, pecans, and pineapple.

3. Chill until the consistency of unbeaten egg whites. Stir to redistribute ingredients. Pour into a lightly greased mold. Chill until firm.

4. Prepare a bed of herb greens on a serving platter. Unmold salad onto greens. Serve with mayonnaise.

Yield: 20 servings

This is a wonderful salad for a holiday celebration.

Green Bean and Carrot Salad

1. Combine sugar, vinegar, and oil. Stir until sugar dissolves.

2. Mix in beans and carrots. Add basil, garlic, salt, and pepper.

3. Refrigerate 1 to 2 hours.

Yield: 4 to 6 servings

Add other vegetables, if desired, such as cauliflower or broccoli flowerets. Steam fresh vegetables 5 minutes or until crisp-tender.

¾ cup sugar
¾ cup herb vinegar of choice
⅓ cup oil
3 (14½-ounce) cans green beans, drained
1 (16-ounce) package frozen sliced carrots, thawed
Chopped fresh basil
1 clove garlic, minced
Salt and pepper to taste

Mardi Gras Salad

1. Blanch and drain peas. Combine peas and next 4 ingredients.

2. Mix together vinegar, oil, and Italian seasoning. Pour over vegetables and mix. If made in advance, retain color by not adding cabbage until just before serving.

Yield: 8 to 10 servings

1 (10-ounce) package frozen green peas
1 (15¼-ounce) can corn, drained
2 cups chopped red cabbage
1 cup chopped celery
1 cup chopped onion
⅓ cup wine vinegar
⅔ cup olive oil
1 teaspoon Italian seasoning

Winter

Side Dishes

Dilled Beet Casserole

2   (16-ounce) cans beets, drained
2   tablespoons margarine
1   tablespoon all-purpose flour
1   teaspoon seasoned salt
1   teaspoon dried dill, or 1 tablespoon fresh, chopped
½   cup light or fat free sour cream
Dash of salt
½   teaspoon black pepper
½   cup buttered breadcrumbs

1. Place beets in a greased shallow casserole dish.

2. In a saucepan, melt margarine. Blend in flour. Heat and stir until mixture is bubbly.

3. Mix in seasoned salt and next 4 ingredients. Pour sauce over beets. Top with breadcrumbs.

4. Cover dish and bake at 350° for 45 minutes.

Yield: 6 to 8 servings

Use diced, sliced, or baby canned beets. Add extra sour cream to sauce, if desired.

To make bouquet garnis for soups and stews, fill 4-inch squares of cheesecloth with herbs, such as thyme, parsley, dill, basil, celery leaves, and marjoram. Tie with a long thread for easy removal from stew.

Christmas Broccoli Mixture

1. Steam broccoli. Place in a 4-quart casserole dish coated with nonstick cooking spray.

2. Sauté mushrooms in 1 tablespoon butter until tender. Add parsley. Combine with broccoli in dish.

3. In a large saucepan, melt 1 stick of butter over low heat. Add flour and blend to a smooth paste. Increase to medium heat and slowly add milk. Stir until sauce thickens.

4. Mix in 2 cups cheese and continue cooking until cheese melts. Season with pepper. Pour over vegetable mixture.

5. Melt remaining 3 tablespoons butter in a large skillet. Sauté onion until tender. Add turkey, bread, and poultry seasoning. Mix well. Distribute over cheese sauce. Sprinkle with remaining 2 cups cheese.

6. Bake at 350° for 55 to 60 minutes.

Yield: 12 *servings*

4 (10-ounce) packages frozen broccoli
8 ounces mushrooms, sliced
1½ sticks butter, divided
1 teaspoon chopped fresh parsley
½ cup whole wheat flour
1 quart milk
4 cups grated Cheddar cheese, divided
Black pepper to taste
2 large onions, finely chopped
2 cups chopped cooked turkey or chicken
½ loaf whole grain bread, crumbled
1 tablespoon poultry seasoning

Winter

Green Pea, Artichoke, and Mushroom Casserole

1 (16-ounce)
   package frozen
   green peas
1 (14-ounce) can
   artichoke hearts,
   drained and sliced
1-2 (4-ounce) cans
   mushroom,
   drained
Fresh or dried sweet
   marjoram or basil
Italian-style
   breadcrumbs
Olive oil

1. Spread half of peas in a greased casserole dish. Layer half of artichokes over peas. Spread half of mushrooms over artichoke. Sprinkle lightly with marjoram and bread-crumbs.

2. Repeat vegetable layers. Season lightly with marjoram. Add a generous layer of bread-crumbs. Drizzle oil over top.

3. Bake uncovered at 375° for 30 minutes or until lightly browned.

Yield: 6 to 8 servings

Serve this dish at holiday meals. Prepare it ahead of time and refrigerate until ready to bake.

Dried-Fruit Ornaments

Materials needed: Green satin ribbon ¼ inch wide, cut into 5-inch strips, dried fruit slices (oranges and apples), Elmer's glue (or hot glue gun)
1. Loop ribbon in half.
2. Hold ends together, and place between 2 slices of fruit.
3. Glue fruit slices together

making sure to secure ribbon with glue.
4. When dry, hang on Christmas tree. Note: Very colorful addition to tree. Smells good too! You may combine apples/oranges, or just apples/apples, oranges/oranges. (Or glue cinnamon bits and allspice onto slices for more fragrance.)

Green and Yellow Rice

1. Cook spinach according to package. Drain.

2. Combine milk and egg. Stir in cheese and spinach, mixing well but gently.

3. Add onion and next 5 ingredients.

4. In a separate bowl, combine margarine and rice. Stir in cheese mixture. Pour into a 2-quart casserole dish. Set dish in a pan of warm water.

5. Bake uncovered at 350° for 45 minutes.

Yield: 10 servings

1	(10-ounce) package frozen chopped spinach
1	cup milk
4	eggs, beaten
1	pound sharp Cheddar cheese, grated
1	tablespoon chopped onion
1	tablespoon Worcestershire sauce
½	teaspoon dried marjoram
½	teaspoon dried thyme
½	teaspoon dried rosemary
½	teaspoon salt
4	tablespoons margarine, melted
3	cups cooked rice

Many Greeks used mint to perfume the bath or to revive someone from a faint.

Winter

Herbal Rice With Yellow Squash

½ cup chopped onion
1 cup chopped celery
4 tablespoons butter, margarine or olive oil, divided
1 cup uncooked rice
½ cup dry white wine
2¼ cups chicken broth
Salt to taste
8 3- to 4-inch herb sprigs of choice
3 cups sliced crookneck squash
½ teaspoon hot pepper sauce
¼ cup lime or lemon juice
¼ cup chopped fresh herbs, including parsley

1. Sauté onion and celery in 2 tablespoons butter, being careful not to brown. Mix in rice and wine. Cook, stirring constantly, until most of wine evaporates.

2. Add broth, salt, and herb sprigs. Bring to a boil and cover. Reduce heat and cook until rice is tender. Remove sprigs.

3. While rice cooks, sauté squash in remaining 2 tablespoons butter. Add squash to rice. Mix in hot pepper sauce, lime or lemon juice, and chopped herbs.

Yield: 6 to 8 servings

Suggested herbs include: thyme, oregano, marjoram, mint marigold, tarragon, basil, sage, or savory. Other vegetables such as broccoli, asparagus, green beans, snow peas, or green peas are good substitutions for squash.

Lentils, Rosemary, and Oregano Over Rice

1. Soak lentils 4 hours minimum in cold water. Drain, rinse, and drain again.

2. Heat olive oil in a large stainless-steel pan over medium heat. Add ham and next 5 ingredients and sauté for 5 minutes.

3. Add lentils, tomato sauce, and enough water to cover. Bring mixture to a boil. Reduce heat and cover. Simmer 45 minutes or until lentils are tender, adding more water if necessary. Season with salt and pepper. Serve over rice.

Yield: 6 to 8 servings

This hearty dish can help "warm the soul" on a cold winter day.

1 pound dried lentils
1 tablespoon olive oil
¼ pound ham, chopped
1 tablespoon fresh rosemary leaves, chopped
2 tablespoons fresh Greek oregano, chopped
2 cloves garlic, minced
1 onion, chopped
2 carrots, peeled and chopped
8 ounces tomato sauce
Salt and pepper
Cooked rice

Pomanders

Peel small strips around oranges, lemons, or limes about ½ inch thick. Place cloves along those strips. Use as decorations in a bowl or placed on the Christmas tree.

Winter

Vegetable Casserole With Lemon Basil

1 (2.8-ounce) can French fried onions, divided
1 (9-ounce) package frozen cut green beans
1 (9-ounce) package frozen mixed vegetables
¾ cup milk
1 (10¾-ounce) can condensed cream of mushroom soup
⅛ teaspoon black pepper
3 tablespoons chopped fresh lemon basil

1. Combine half of onions with remaining 6 ingredients. Pour mixture into a 1½-quart casserole dish.

2. Bake uncovered at 350° for 30 minutes or until fully heated. Top with remaining onions and bake 5 minutes or until onions appear golden brown.

Yield: 6 to 8 servings

A handful of lemon verbena leaves left to infuse a teapot of very hot water for 5 minutes becomes a wonderful finale to a rather large meal.

Main Dishes

Deep-Dish Breakfast Pizza

1. Cook and drain sausage. Press rolls into a deep-dish pizza pan. Spread sausage on top. Sprinkle with sage and Cheddar cheese.

2. Beat eggs, milk, salt, and pepper together. Pour over Cheddar cheese. Sprinkle with Parmesan cheese.

3. Bake at 350° for 20 minutes or until done.

Yield: 6 to 8 servings

1 pound sausage
1 (8-ounce) can refrigerated crescent rolls
1 tablespoon chopped fresh sage
2 cups grated Cheddar cheese
5 eggs
¼ cup milk
Salt and pepper to taste
Parmesan cheese for topping

Winter

Christmas Morning Cheese Casserole

10 slices herb or regular bread, crusts removed
4 tablespoons butter, melted
2 cups grated extra sharp Cheddar cheese
1 teaspoon dry mustard
1 teaspoon salt
¼ teaspoon paprika
1 teaspoon dried dill
4 eggs, beaten
3 cups light cream

1. Place bread in a 13x9x2-inch casserole dish. Combine butter and remaining 7 ingredients. Pour over bread. Refrigerate overnight.

2. Top with extra cheese, if desired, before baking. Bake at 350° for 45 minutes.

Yield: 6 to 8 servings

Bake this Christmas morning while opening presents. Serve with fruit, grits, and ham and biscuits. Vary recipe by adding cooked and crumbled sausage or ham.

Spicy Citrus Potpourri

3 cups dried orange slices
3 cups dried lemon slices
3 cups dried apple slices
2 cups dried cranberries
2 cups dried rose hips
½ cup whole cloves
2 cups (1-inch pieces) cinnamon sticks
1 cup whole star anise
2 cups whole nutmeg

1 cup whole allspice
½ cup sliced or dried ginger
½ cup whole cardamom
10 drops orange oil
10 drops citrus oil

Mix all ingredients gently. Store in glass jars with tight fitting lids for 3 weeks. Display in attractive bowls, baskets, or other containers to scent your house for the holidays.

Fettuccini Carbonara

1. Cook fettuccini according to package.
Drain and keep warm.

2. Cook bacon until crisp. Crumble. Combine
cheeses.

3. Sauté onion, bell pepper, and mushrooms
in 2 tablespoons butter until onion browns.
Add wine and simmer 10 to 12 minutes. If
needed, add a small amount of extra hot wine
or hot water to moisten mixture before
adding to noodles.

4. Melt remaining 4 tablespoons butter and
pour over fettuccini. Add egg and mix. Add
cheeses and mix thoroughly. Stir in bacon
and vegetables. Add parsley and mix well.

Yield: 4 servings

Serve with a tossed salad, garlic bread, and additional
cheese on the side.

1 (8-ounce) package fettuccini
12 ounces bacon
⅓ cup grated Romano cheese
⅓ cup Parmesan cheese
¾ cup chopped green onion
¾ cup chopped bell pepper
1 (4-ounce) can mushrooms, drained and chopped
6 tablespoons butter, divided
¾ cup dry white wine
1 egg, lightly beaten
¼ cup chopped fresh parsley

Herb Tray

Keep your seed packets and glue them on a metal tray. Cover with two coats of
polyurethane.

Rosemary Pepper Pasta

⅔ cup olive oil
½ cup rosemary vinegar
Juice of 1 lemon
3 tablespoons fresh rosemary
16 ounces penne pasta
1 bell pepper, julienne
1 red bell pepper, julienne
Freshly ground black pepper
16 ounces cooked medium shrimp, peeled

1. Combine oil and next 3 ingredients to make a marinade. Cook pasta according to package directions. Drain.

2. Combine pasta, half the marinade, and bell peppers. Sprinkle with a generous amount of black pepper.

3. In a separate bowl, mix shrimp and remaining marinade. Refrigerate both mixtures overnight.

4. To serve, combine shrimp and pasta mixture. Sprinkle with black pepper.

Yield: 6 to 8 servings

Substitute any white wine or herbal vinegar if rosemary vinegar is not available. Make the marinade in one step; then use separately to marinate the pasta and shrimp.

Crabmeat Entree

1 (6-ounce) can crabmeat, flaked
1 (10¾-ounce) can condensed cream of mushroom soup
Juice of ½ lemon
¼ teaspoon dried marjoram

1. Combine all ingredients in the top of a double boiler. Heat.

2. Serve on Melba toast or toasted bread.

Yield: 3 or 4 servings

This quick and easy recipe is good as a luncheon dish.

Winter

Crabmeat, Pasta, and Pesto

1. Cook rotini according to package.

2. While pasta cooks, sauté green onions and bell pepper in butter in a large skillet. Add mushrooms, olives, and crabmeat and warm slightly.

3. When tender, drain pasta. Add hot pasta and pesto to vegetables. Toss to coat pasta thoroughly. Add black pepper and top with cheese. Serve hot or cold.

Yield: 4 to 6 servings

Use any fresh vegetables in place of, or in addition to, the onions and bell pepper. Substitute white wine for butter to reduce fat.

The savory basil paste called pesto is presented in an unusual way in this recipe.

1 (8-ounce) package rotini pasta
1 bunch green onions, chopped
1 bell pepper, chopped
2 tablespoons butter or olive oil
1 (7-ounce) can mushrooms, drained
1 (2¼-ounce) can sliced black olives, drained
1 (16-ounce) package imitation lump crabmeat
¾ cup basil pesto
Freshly ground black pepper to taste
½ cup freshly grated Romano cheese

Salmon Puff

1. Beat eggs until light. Mix in milk and cracker.

2. Drain salmon. Discard bones and dark skin. Crumble salmon into egg mixture. Add parsley, tarragon, and thyme. Mix well.

3. Pour into a greased, shallow 1½- or 2-quart baking dish. Bake at 350° for 40 minutes or until a knife inserted near the center comes out clean.

Yield: 6 to 8 servings

4 eggs
2 cups milk
1 cup finely ground unsalted saltine crackers or matzo
1 (15-ounce) can red salmon
¼ cup chopped fresh parsley
¼ teaspoon dried tarragon
¼ teaspoon ground thyme

Today's Herbal Kitchen 219

Winter

Syracuse Salmon

Sour Cream Dressing

- ½ cup sour cream
- 1 tablespoon fresh or dried dill
- 2 tablespoons lemon juice

Fish

- 2 salmon steaks or fillets
- 2 tablespoons olive oil
- ¾ cup white wine
- 2 tablespoons fresh onion chives
- 2 tablespoons fresh lemon thyme or lemon balm
- 2 tablespoons fresh tarragon
- 2 tablespoons fresh dill

1. To make sour cream dressing, combine sour cream, dill, and lemon juice.

2. Prepare fish by sautéing salmon in oil until lightly browned on each side. Add wine and remaining 4 ingredients. Cook about 7 to 10 minutes on each side. Serve with dressing.

Yield: 2 servings

 White willow bark tea is instant relief for a sore throat.

Shrimp Bordelaise

1. Peel and devein shrimp, leaving last segment of shell and tail intact. Melt butter in a large skillet over medium heat. Add garlic and next 4 ingredients. Bring to a boil.

2. Add shrimp and cook, uncovered, 5 minutes or until shrimp turns bright pink. Using a slotted spoon, remove shrimp to a serving dish and keep warm. Rapidly boil down liquid in skillet until reduced to about ½ cup. Mix in parsley. Pour over shrimp. Serve with noodles or rice pilaf and cheese.

Yield: 4 to 6 servings

Use pre-cooked, frozen shrimp with tails, if desired. Reduce cooking time after adding shrimp to 3 minutes.

Peel shrimp immediately before tossing into garlic butter for freshest taste and food safety.

1½ pounds large fresh shrimp
3 tablespoons butter or margarine
3 cloves garlic, minced
1 bunch green onions including stems, finely chopped
1½ tablespoons lemon juice
1 teaspoon fresh lemon thyme, or ¼ teaspoon dried
1 cup white wine
3 tablespoons minced fresh parsley
Cooked vermicelli noodles or rice pilaf
Parmesan cheese

Emma's Beef Stew

6 cups water, divided

4 beef bouillon cubes

2½ pounds lean beef, cubed

1 large dried bay leaf

½ teaspoon salt

¼ teaspoon black pepper

⅛ teaspoon dried oregano

1 teaspoon dried parsley

⅛ teaspoon dried rosemary

⅛ teaspoon dried thyme

1 medium onion, thinly sliced

1 medium bell pepper, diced

6 medium carrots, cubed

6 medium potatoes, cubed

½ cup all-purpose flour

1. Bring 2 cups water to a boil. Add bouillon cubes and stir to dissolve.

2. In a large Dutch oven, bring remaining 4 cups water to a boil. Add bouillon to water.

3. Sear beef in a skillet. Add to Dutch oven. Mix in bay leaf and next 8 ingredients. Simmer 2 hours.

4. Add carrot and potato. Simmer 30 minutes.

5. Combine flour with enough water to make a paste. Add paste to stew. Simmer 30 minutes longer. Remove bay leaf.

Yield: 8 servings

If cooking time is limited, prepare half of stew ahead. Simmer beef, seasonings, onion, and bell pepper for 60 minutes. Refrigerate. When ready to finish stew, add carrot and potato and cook as directed.

Herb Burger Cups

1. Brown beef and drain. Add salsa and next 3 ingredients. Mix well.

2. Separate dough into biscuits. Flatten and place in ungreased muffin cups. Press dough up sides to edge of cups. Spoon beef mixture into cups. Sprinkle with cheese.

3. Bake at 400° for 10 minutes or until crust is brown.

Yield: 10 to 12 cups

Bake the burger right into the bun.

¾ pound ground round
½ cup salsa
1 teaspoon dried thyme
1 teaspoon dried basil
1 teaspoon dried parsley
1 (10- to 12-ounce) can flaky-style refrigerated biscuits
¾ cup grated sharp Cheddar cheese

Herbed Roast Beef

1. Place roast in a casserole dish coated with nonstick cooking spray.

2. Combine garlic powder and remaining 4 ingredients. Sprinkle mixture over roast. Add ½ inch water to bottom of dish.

3. Cover and bake at 300° for 4 to 5 hours or until tender. Slice and serve au jus.

Yield: 8 to 10 servings

This is a great do-ahead main dish.

1 (4-pound) boneless chuck or rump roast
½ teaspoon garlic powder
1½ teaspoons dried oregano
1½ teaspoons crushed dried rosemary
½ teaspoon freshly ground black pepper
1 tablespoon beef bouillon

Chicken Rice Paprikash

6 chicken breasts or
thighs, boned and
skinned
4 tablespoons
paprika
2 tablespoons salt
½ large onion, diced
8 cups water
1½ cups uncooked
brown rice
⅓ cup fresh
rosemary
⅓ cup fresh thyme
1 carrot, cut into
strips
1 stalk celery with
leaves, sliced
⅓ cup fresh parsley

1. Combine chicken and next 4 ingredients in a large Dutch oven. Bring to a boil. Add rice and next 4 ingredients. Stir well. Cover and cook on medium-low heat for 50 minutes. Stir occasionally and add extra water as needed.

2. Near end of cooking time, uncover to allow excess water to evaporate and add parsley.

Yield: 6 servings

Cinnamon People

Materials needed: 2 cups applesauce, 2 cups ground cinnamon (extra for cutting out), tiny gingerbread man cutter.
1. Mix half cinnamon and half applesauce in bowl.
2. Slightly grease hands and pat mixture into a ball.
3. Sprinkle extra cinnamon on flat surface as for "rolling out" biscuits.
4. Pinch off baseball-size chunk of dough and roll to ¼ inch thick.
5. Cut out with gingerbread man (and woman) cookie cutters. Punch hole in head with ice pick.
6. Let dry on wax paper for several days turning once a day. String on ribbon or twine.

Paella

1. Heat oil in a Dutch oven or a large paella pan. Add chicken and pork and cook about 15 minutes.

2. Remove meat from pan. Add onion and garlic to pan. Cook until onion is tender. Drain fat.

3. Stir in chicken broth and next 7 ingredients. Add chicken and pork and heat to a boil. Transfer to an oven and bake, uncovered, at 350° for 20 minutes.

4. Remove from oven. Stir in shrimp. Tuck mussels into rice with opening-side up. Stir in peas. Bake 10 to 15 minutes or until mussels open and shrimp turn pink and opaque. Garnish with pimiento.

Yield: 8 to 10 servings

This Spanish classic is worth the effort for a lively gathering—perhaps a Super Bowl Sunday buffet.

¼ cup olive oil
1 pound chicken breasts, boned and cut into large pieces
1 pound chicken thighs, boned
1 meaty pork chop, diced
1 medium onion, sliced
1 clove garlic, chopped
4 cups chicken broth
1½ cups uncooked rice
1 (15-ounce) can tomatoes, undrained
2 teaspoons salt
1 tablespoon paprika
½ teaspoon black pepper
⅛ teaspoon saffron
½ teaspoon cayenne pepper
1 pound raw shrimp, peeled and deveined
2 pounds mussels or clams, cleaned
1 (10-ounce) package frozen peas
1 (2-ounce) jar sliced pimientos

Winter

Stuffed Tenderloin

4 tablespoons minced garlic, divided
2 bell peppers, thinly sliced
2 red bell peppers, thinly sliced
2 onions, thinly sliced
2 tablespoons fresh rosemary
2 tablespoons fresh thyme
2 tablespoons fresh marjoram
¼ cup olive oil
1½ pounds beef or pork tenderloin
1 cup red wine
½ cup Worcestershire sauce
2 tablespoons Greek seasoning

1. Sauté 2 tablespoons garlic and next 6 ingredients in oil until tender. Cool.

2. Slice tenderloin down the center without cutting through completely. Place vegetable mixture in the center. Roll tenderloin together and tie ends and center with string.

3. Combine wine, Worcestershire sauce, and remaining 2 tablespoons garlic. Marinate tenderloin in mixture for 2 hours. Remove tenderloin from marinade and rub with Greek seasoning.

4. Bake at 400° for 20 to 30 minutes per pound or until meat is pink in the center. Slice.

Yield: 6 to 8 servings

Cooking tenderloin on a grill is equally good.

Herbed Roast Leg of Lamb With Vegetables

1. Whip together mustard, salt, pepper, and next 6 ingredients.

2. Prepare lamb by removing papery outer covering and visible fat. Brush half of mustard mixture over entire leg. Marinate in refrigerator overnight.

3. Bring lamb to room temperature. Place in a greased roasting pan. Brush with remaining marinade, pouring any extra over top. Bake at 400° for 10 minutes. Reduce heat to 325° and cook 20 to 30 minutes per pound of meat.

4. Using a thermometer, cook to desired degree of doneness. Do not overcook. Steam onions, carrot, and potatoes. Add vegetables to roast during last hour of cooking. Baste vegetables with pan juices.

5. When done baking, transfer lamb to a serving platter and let stand 20 minutes before carving. Pour pan drippings into a saucepan. Keep vegetables warm in roasting pan until serving time.

6. Make a gravy by adding red wine and broth to pan drippings. Mix flour with enough water to make a thin paste. Bring broth to a boil. Mix some of hot broth into flour paste, then add back into saucepan. Cook and stir until gravy reaches desired thickness.

7. When ready to serve, remove string from lamb and carve into slices. Surround slices with vegetables. Garnish. Serve gravy on the side.

Yield: 12 to 16 servings

½   cup Dijon mustard
Salt and pepper to taste
5   cloves garlic, pressed
2   tablespoons chopped dried rosemary
1   teaspoon dried thyme
1   teaspoon dried oregano
1   cup dry white wine
2   tablespoons olive oil
1   (5- or 6-pound) leg of lamb, boned and tied
12 small onions
6   carrots, cut into 2-inch pieces
8   potatoes, halved if large
1   cup red wine
2   cups beef broth
3   tablespoons quick mixing, all-purpose flour
Sprigs of fresh rosemary for garnish

Winter

Chicken Cacciatore

Cacciatore

- 1 frying chicken, cut in pieces
- ¼ cup olive oil
- 2 onions, sliced
- 2 cloves garlic, crushed
- 1 (14½-ounce) can tomatoes, undrained
- 1 (8-ounce) can tomato sauce
- ½ teaspoon salt
- 1 teaspoon dried oregano
- 2 dried bay leaves
- 1 (7-ounce) can sliced mushrooms, drained
- 1 (10-ounce) package frozen green peas

Herbed Rice

- 1 cup uncooked rice
- 2 cups cold water
- 2 teaspoons chicken bouillon
- ½ teaspoon crushed fresh or dried rosemary
- ½ teaspoon dried marjoram, or 1 tablespoon fresh
- ½ teaspoon dried thyme, or 1 tablespoon fresh

1. Remove chicken skin, if desired. Brown chicken in oil in a large deep skillet; then remove.

2. Add onion and garlic to skillet and sauté until lightly browned. Add tomatoes and next 5 ingredients. Simmer 5 minutes. Add chicken and cover. Simmer 45 minutes or until chicken is tender. Add peas during last 5 minutes of cooking time.

3. To make herbed rice, combine rice and remaining 5 ingredients in a heavy saucepan. Bring to a boil over high heat. Reduce to medium-low heat, stir, and cover. Simmer 12 to 14 minutes or until all liquid is absorbed. If using a microwave, place rice and remaining ingredients in a greased 2-quart casserole dish. Cook on high power 2 minutes. Lower power and simmer 18 minutes. Stir lightly. Serve herbed rice with chicken cacciatore.

Yield: 4 servings

Chicken Campania

1. Sauté chicken livers in butter until they just lose their pinkness. Remove to a small bowl. Add anchovy and mash into a paste.

2. Combine flour, salt, and pepper. Dredge chicken in flour mixture; set aside.

3. Heat oil over medium heat in a large skillet. Add garlic and sauté until lightly browned. Discard garlic. Add chicken to skillet and brown all sides.

4. Add liver mixture, green onions, and next 8 ingredients. Mix well and cover. Simmer 20 minutes over low heat, stirring occasionally. Uncover and cook 15 minutes longer, or until sauce is thickened and chicken is tender.

5. Serve with cheese sprinkled on top and sauce spooned over spaghetti.

Yield: 6 servings

5 chicken livers
1 tablespoon butter
1 anchovy fillet, rinsed
¼ cup all-purpose flour
½ teaspoon salt
¼ teaspoon freshly ground black pepper
1 (2½- to 3-pound) chicken, cut up and skinned
6 tablespoons extra virgin olive oil
2 cloves garlic, sliced
3 green onions, chopped
1 small carrot, grated
1 stalk celery, chopped
1 (28-ounce) can Italian-style tomatoes
1 teaspoon chopped fresh basil, or ¼ teaspoon crumbled dried
¾ teaspoon chopped fresh sage, or ¼ teaspoon crumbled dried
¼ teaspoon crumbled dried oregano
Pinch of crumbled fresh or dried rosemary
½ cup chicken broth
Grated imported Romano cheese
Hot cooked spaghetti

Winter

Chicken Rolls

4 chicken breasts, boned and skinned
4 thin slices boiled ham
4 thin slices Swiss cheese
1 (10-ounce) package frozen chopped spinach, thawed and drained
4 tablespoons butter
4 tablespoons all-purpose flour
2 cups milk
1 teaspoon minced fresh parsley
1 tablespoon chopped fresh chives
1 teaspoon dried thyme

1. With a mallet, flatten breasts to about ¼ inch thick. Place a slice of ham and a slice of cheese on each breast. Divide spinach between breasts. Roll breasts, starting at the small end. Secure with toothpicks.

2. Place in a baking dish, seam side down. Melt butter in a saucepan. Blend in flour slowly to prevent lumps. Cook and stir constantly while gradually adding milk.

3. When sauce thickens, mix in parsley, chives, and thyme. Pour sauce over chicken and cover. Bake at 350° for about 60 minutes. Uncover during last 5 to 10 minutes of cooking time.

Yield: 4 servings

Place fresh or dried herbs along with lemon slices in the cavity of chicken or rock Cornish game hens before baking.

Marge's Company Casserole

1. Cook beans for 1 minute in boiling water. Cool with running water and drain.

2. Season chicken with salt and pepper. Combine stuffing and next 3 ingredients.

3. Coat a 14x10x2-inch casserole dish with nonstick cooking spray. Spread 2 cups of stuffing mix on bottom of dish. Layer beans, almonds, and chicken on top. Blend soup and milk and pour over chicken.

4. Combine remaining stuffing mix with hot water and butter. Spread over top of casserole. Bake at 325° for 45 minutes.

Yield: 8 to 10 servings

1 (20-ounce) package frozen French-cut green beans
4 cups cooked and diced chicken or turkey
Salt and pepper
6 cups dry cornbread stuffing
1 tablespoon fresh basil
1 tablespoon fresh parsley
1 teaspoon fresh thyme
1 cup slivered almonds, toasted
2 (10-ounce) cans creamed onion soup
1 cup milk
⅔ cup hot water
6 tablespoons butter or margarine, melted

Winter

Roasted Tarragon Chicken

1 (2- to 3-pound) roasting chicken
2 tablespoons margarine, softened
1 lemon, cut into wedges
1 tablespoon dried tarragon
¼ teaspoon black pepper
⅓ cup white wine
1 clove garlic, or garlic powder
1 cup water

1. Clean chicken. Spread margarine over entire surface of chicken, especially the legs and breast. Rub cut surfaces of lemon wedges over chicken. Place wedges in chicken cavity. Sprinkle tarragon and pepper on top and in cavity of chicken. Place in a roasting pan. Pour wine in cavity. Add garlic to cavity. Pour water in pan and cover.

2. Bake at 350° for about 45 minutes. Uncover and bake about 30 minutes longer.

Yield: 4 to 6 servings

Sesame Drumettes

3 pounds chicken wings
1 cup soy sauce
½ cup lemon juice
1 clove garlic, crushed
¼ teaspoon fresh ginger
Sesame seeds

1. Remove wing tips and discard. Cut each wing at the joint to separate into 2 sections. Wash and pat dry.

2. Combine soy sauce and next 3 ingredients. Pour over wings. Marinate 30 minutes or overnight in the refrigerator. Drain wings and discard marinade.

3. Place wings on a rack in a broiler pan or a glass baking dish. Sprinkle generously with sesame seeds.

4. Broil 15 minutes; then bake at 400° for 30 minutes.

Yield: 4 to 6 servings

Desserts

Christmas Pie

1. Place pecan pieces and chocolate chips in bottom of pie crust.

2. Beat together whiskey and next 7 ingredients. Pour over pecan pieces and chocolate chips.

3. Bake at 350° for 45 minutes. Serve with whipped cream sprinkled with garnish.

Yield: 8 servings

½ cup pecan pieces
½ cup chocolate chips
1 unbaked 9-inch pie shell
4 tablespoons whiskey
4 tablespoons butter, melted
½ cup sugar
1 tablespoon all-purpose flour
3 eggs
½ cup pancake syrup
1 teaspoon vanilla
⅛ teaspoon salt
Fresh rosemary for garnish

For a tasty sauce for cheese omelets or on rice, mince 1/4 cup fresh hyssop, and add to 4 cups tomato sauce.

Winter

Cranberry Pumpkin Bread

2 eggs, lightly beaten
2 cups sugar
½ cup oil
1 cup canned pumpkin
2¼ cups all-purpose flour
1 tablespoon pumpkin pie spice
1 teaspoon baking soda
½ teaspoon salt
1 cup chopped cranberries

1. Combine egg and next 3 ingredients. Mix well.

2. Combine flour and next 3 ingredients in a large bowl. Form a well in the center of dry ingredients. Pour pumpkin mixture into well. Blend to just moisten dry ingredients. Stir in cranberries.

3. Spoon batter into 2 greased and floured 8x4x2½-inch aluminum loaf pans. Bake at 350° for 60 minutes or until a toothpick inserted near the center comes out clean.

Yield: 2 loaves

Lemon Cranberry Loaf

5 tablespoons margarine
1 (8-ounce) package cream cheese, softened
1¼ cups sugar
1 teaspoon vanilla
3 eggs
2 tablespoons lemon juice
1 teaspoon lemon zest
1½ cups chopped cranberries
2¼ cups all-purpose flour
2 teaspoons baking powder
½ teaspoon baking soda

1. Combine margarine and next 3 ingredients in a large mixing bowl. Cream with an electric mixer at medium speed until well blended. Add eggs one at a time, mixing well after each addition. Stir in lemon juice and zest.

2. Toss cranberries and remaining 3 ingredients together in a large bowl. Add cream cheese mixture and blend until just moistened.

3. Pour into a greased and floured 9x5x3-inch loaf pan. Bake at 325° for 1 hour, 15 minutes. Cool 5 minutes. Remove from pan and cool completely. Garnish with extra lemon zest, if desired.

Yield: 1 loaf

Capriland's Triple-Seed Holiday Cake

1. Sift together flour and next 3 ingredients.

2. In a separate bowl, cream shortening and sugar. Add eggs one at a time, beating about 1 minute after each addition. Blend in lemon zest.

3. Gradually add dry ingredient mixture and milk, alternately, to creamed mixture. Mix well. Spread a quarter of batter into a greased and floured tube pan. Sprinkle with caraway seed. Pour in another quarter of batter. Sprinkle with poppy seed. Add half of remaining batter. Sprinkle with anise seed. Top with remaining batter.

4. Bake at 350° for about 1 hour, 20 minutes. Cool on a rack 15 minutes. Remove from pan. Cool. Sprinkle with powdered sugar, or frost if desired.

Yield: 10 to 12 servings

This is a delicious recipe to take to a holiday potluck.

3 cups all-purpose flour
2½ teaspoons baking powder
¾ teaspoon nutmeg
1 teaspoon salt
⅔ cup shortening
2 cups sugar
4 eggs
3 tablespoons lemon zest
1 cup milk
1 tablespoon caraway seed
1 tablespoon poppy seed
1 teaspoon anise seed
Powdered sugar for topping

Winter

Christmas Cookies

5 cups all-purpose flour
1½ cups sugar
2 teaspoons salt
2 cups shortening
2 teaspoons vanilla
½ cup evaporated milk
1 tablespoon crushed dried mint
5 egg yolks
2 egg whites
1 teaspoon water
Nuts and colored sugar for topping

1. Combine flour, sugar, and salt. Cut in shortening. Add vanilla and next 3 ingredients. Mix to form stiff dough.

2. Roll out and cut into shapes using cookie cutters. Place cookies on a baking sheet.

3. Beat together egg whites and water until frothy. Brush over cookies. Sprinkle with nuts and colored sugar. Bake at 350° for 8 to 10 minutes.

Yield: 4 to 5 dozen

This family favorite dates back many years, with mint being added to the recipe only recently.

Rosemary Treats

¾ cup packed light brown sugar
2 eggs, beaten
½ teaspoon vanilla
1 cup all-purpose flour
1 teaspoon baking powder
½ teaspoon salt
1 tablespoon fresh rosemary leaves
4 ounces white raisins
4 ounces candied cherries and pineapple mixture
1 cup chopped pecans

1. Combine sugar, egg, and vanilla and mix well.

2. Sift together flour, baking powder, and salt. Gradually add to egg mixture. Sprinkle with rosemary leaves. Fold in raisins, cherries and pineapple mixture, and pecans.

3. Spread evenly into a greased and floured 8-inch square pan. Bake at 375° for 30 minutes. Remove from pan and cool before slicing.

Yield: 6 to 8 servings

Three-in-one Cookies

Basic Cookie Mix

1	cup shortening
1	cup sugar
1	cup packed brown sugar
2	cups all-purpose flour
1	teaspoon baking powder
¼	teaspoon salt
1	teaspoon cinnamon
2	cups quick-cooking rolled oats
2	cups crushed corn flakes

Orange Cookies

2	cups basic cookie mix
1	egg, lightly beaten
3	tablespoons orange zest
1	tablespoon orange juice
1	tablespoon chopped fresh orange mint
½	cup chopped pecans

1. To make basic cookie mix, cream shortening and sugars. Add flour and next 5 ingredients. Blend well. Cover and refrigerate until ready to use.

2. To make orange cookies, combine all ingredients. Shape into 1-inch balls. Place 2 inches apart on an ungreased baking sheet.

3. Bake at 375° for 10 to 12 minutes.

Yield: 8 cups basic cookie mix, 2½ dozen orange cookies

Variations: To make Lemon Cookies, substitute lemon zest for orange zest, lemon juice for orange juice, and chopped fresh lemon balm for orange mint.

To make Apple Cookies, substitute 1 tablespoon sesame seed for orange zest, apple juice for orange juice, and chopped fresh apple mint for orange mint.

Winter

Rosemary Pecan Biscotti

2¼ cups all-purpose flour
1 teaspoon baking powder
1 cup sugar
2 tablespoons stone-ground cornmeal
1 teaspoon salt
1 egg
½ cup plain low fat yogurt
1 stick margarine, softened
1 cup coarsely chopped pecans, toasted
¼ cup chopped fresh rosemary, or 1½ tablespoons crumbled dried

1. Blend flour and next 4 ingredients with an electric mixer. Add egg and yogurt. Beat on low speed until mixture forms a dough.

2. Cut margarine into small pieces and mix into dough until just blended. Stir in pecans and rosemary.

3. Place dough on a lightly floured surface. Knead several times, cover with a towel, and let stand 5 minutes.

4. Cut dough in half. Working on a greased and floured jellyroll pan with floured hands, form each half into a log 12 to 15 inches long. Flatten log until about 2 inches wide. Arrange logs at least 3 inches apart on the pan.

5. Bake at 325° for 20 to 25 minutes or until set and pale golden. Cool on pan on a rack for 10 minutes. Transfer to a cutting board. Cut logs crosswise, on a slant, into ½-inch slices. Arrange slices, cut sides down, on pan.

6. Bake at 325° for about 10 minutes on each side or until pale golden. Place on rack to cool. Store in airtight containers.

Yield: 40 to 50 slices

Cookie Exchange

A Christmas Cookie Exchange keeps on giving even after you've nibbled cookies among friends.

Cookies are shared at home with family and often, tucked into packages to share with still more of our dearest ones.

Steps to a successful cookie exchange begin with inviting your guests.

Give them plenty of time to bake the extra cookies they'll need. Our Christmas cookies with herbs begin on page 236. Ask each guest to bring a half dozen cookies for each guest plus a half dozen cookies for a sneak preview of flavors during refreshment time.

Sharing recipes is a nice touch, too. The guests can collect their cookie cache in cookie tins or plastic bags.

Pass the cookies and you may hear such advice as:

• Unsalted butter gives cookies a fresher flavor.

• Before baking cut cookies, set the baking sheet in the freezer for a few minutes to help cookies hold their shape.

• If baking sheets are warped, cookies may not bake uniformly.

• Cool baking sheets between batches. Otherwise, dough begins to melt and cookies may be misshapen.

Winter

Wreath-Making Tips

The art of making wreaths of greens and flowers is a tradition that stretches back for centuries. An herbal natural addition to your home for any holiday or celebration or for year-round decorations.

There are as many different approaches to wreath making as there are wreath makers, and there is really no right or wrong way. All materials are bound onto either a homemade or a store-bought base. These can be made of straw, wire, or vines. Fresh background material of herbs, such as Silver King Artemisia, sweet annie (artemisia anna), thyme, or sage, is bound to the chosen base by using monofilament fishing line or small floral wire. Fresh material rather than dried is used on the base because it is more pliable and easier to shape to the wreath form. Always allow more base than you think you will use because it shrinks as it dries.

The covered base is allowed to dry and then previously dried flowers and seed pods from your garden are applied to the base with a glue gun.

It is usually easier to glue the large flowers and seed heads on the wreath first, then add the smaller flowers to fill-in around them and complete the wreath.

After it is finished, step back and examine it with a critical eye. If you notice any holes or spaces, go back and tuck in some more flowers. Be sure to add a wire hanger on the back and a ribbon on the front, if you choose.

Your finished wreath takes very little care and should last several years with the proper care. The color of flowers will fade if you hang the wreath in direct sun. The same applies to the fragrance of the herbs. Sunlight breaks down essential oils and they lose their scent.

When not in use, store your wreaths in loose paper bags or boxes in a dark, dry location. Plastic bags will cause condensation. An herb wreath, carefully made, either for yourself or for a gift to others, brings back memories of the garden for years to come.

Contributors

We appreciate all those who contributed recipes, tips, and design ideas to this cookbook. Note those who have one * were members of the cookbook committee. Those with two ** are experts in the field of herbs and have led seminars for the Memphis Herb Society.

Jean Anthony
Verlie Baker*
Gwen Barclay**
Judy M. Barnhardt
Jori Barrach
Peggy W. Bedsworth
Judy Bell*
Ray Bennett
Marjorie Binford
Laura Booth
Catherine Ann Bowling
Elizabeth Bowman
Frances Bradley
Marie Brinn*
Karen Britton
Kathy Brown*
Margaret Brown
Trudy Brown
Barbara Buchanan
Shaw Buhler
Lila Beth Burke
Sara Burnette
Amy Ruth Burt
Theresa Burton*
Jim Cardell
Dixie Carlson
Jane Cook
Sandy Cornelius
Pat Crawford
Lynn Dirga
Sallie Doeg
Frank G. Donofrio
Lynn D. Dudley
Josephine Elosua
Nickii Elrod*

Urania Erskine
Lorraine Ferguson
Jennifer B. Fox
Christine Arpe Gang*
Barbara Gaskin
Isabel Glaser
Debra Ann Morton Grimes
John Grisanti
Dorothy Griscom
Mary Harvey Gurley**
Elaine K. Haas*
Carol Ann Hallam
Elsie Heintz
Dr. Kitsie Hendrix
Monica Hern
Eleanor Herron
Madalene Hill**
Ann Hultz
Myra Humphrey*
Dean Humphreys
Sister Jeanine Jaster
Catherine E. Jones
Cheryl C. Jones
Debby Jones*
Connie Kayser
Nan Lemons
Carolyn Lendermon
Mona R. Lupardus
Mary Ann Main
Katherine Maness
Katherine McCormick
Ann Saunders Miller
Evelyn Mosely*
Angela G. Mullikin*
Dottie Norton

Kim Oakley
Otis Oellerich
Kay Parker
Louise Parker
Bernice Perry
Judy Perry
Helen Putnam*
Fran Ragan
Alice Rhodes
Eone Riales* **
Hannah Russell
Harriet S. Sharp*
Dorothy Scott
Marge Serrill*
Josie Sides**
Adelma Grenier
   Simmons**
Mr. and Mrs. George
   Sisterhen
Bob and Joy Straw
Stephanie Street
Sister Marilyn Terwilliger
Bill Thesmar
Emelie Tolley**
Muriel Vinson
Maria Walls
Danette Watkins
Kenneth Watson
Tina Marie Wilcox**
Janet Williams
Laurie Williams
Jim Wilson**
Cathy Winterburn
Mae Belle Wright
Edna C. York

Index

Index

Index

Index

Index

Index

Index

M

Index

Index

Index

Index

Index

Index

Today's Herbal Kitchen
c/o Wimmer Cookbook Distribution
4210 B. F. Goodrich Boulevard
Memphis, Tennessee 38118

Please send_____ copies of *Today's Herbal Kitchen*

@ $19.95 each_____

Tennessee residents add sales tax @ $ 1.65 each_____

Postage and handling @ $5.00 each_____

Total_____

Charge to Visa (   ) or MasterCard (   )

_____ Expiration Date_____

Signature _____

Name _____

Address _____

City _____ State _____ Zip _____

Cookbook Lovers Take Note...

If you've enjoyed *Today's Herbal Kitchen*, The Wimmer Companies, Inc., has a catalog of 250 other cookbook titles that may interest you. To receive your free copy, write:

The Wimmer Companies, Inc.
4210 B. F. Goodrich Boulevard
Memphis, Tennessee 38118
or
call 1-800-727-1034